BREAKING DOWN WALLS

You, Lord, are my lamp;
the Lord turns my darkness into light.
With your help I can advance against a troop[a];
with my God I can scale a **WALL**.

2 Samuel 22:29-30

BREAKING

DOWN

WALLS

A BATTLE WORTH FIGHTING

CHRISTIAN CHAPMAN

ILLUMIFY
MEDIA.COM

Published by

Illumify Media Global

www.IllumifyMedia.com

"Let's bring your book to life!"

Paperback ISBN: 978-1-964251-33-2

Cover design by Debbie Lewis

Printed in the United States of America

For more about Christian Chapman, visit www.christianchapman.com

CONTENTS

Acknowledgments vii

Chapter 1: Let's Get It On! 1

Chapter 2: A Wall Of Self 19

Chapter 3: A Wall of Insecurity 33

Chapter 4: A Wall of Unforgiveness 47

Chapter 5: A Wall of Complacency 61

Chapter 6: A Wall of Fear 75

Chapter 7: A Wall of Addiction 89

Chapter 8: A Wall of Religion 101

Chapter 9: A Wall of Doubt 115

Chapter 10: A Wall of Racism 129

Chapter 11: A Wall of Disunity 145

Chapter 12: A Wall of Hypocrisy 159

Conclusion: A Wall Has Fallen 173

ACKNOWLEDGMENTS

First and foremost I want to thank my Lord and Savior, Jesus Christ. Without You I obviously wouldn't be writing this book. The more I think about my past failures, ongoing shortcomings, and the walls I have faced in my life, the more my heart is drawn to You. Where else could I find a love that never fails? You are my light in times of darkness, my shelter in the midst of storms, and my best friend when the world rejects me. Thank You for Your love, thank You for Your grace, and thank You for enduring the cross. I love You, my King.

To my beautiful wife, Amy . . . How far we have come since that blind date in 1987! I knew immediately that I wanted to spend the rest of my life with you, and my love for you has grown and deepened with each passing year. Even during difficult or uncertain times, you have been supportive and faithful to the call God has on my life. I look forward to serving our Lord together in the days and seasons to come as we continue to listen for that still, quiet voice to lead us. I love you, baby!

To my three boys, Malachi, Isaiah, and Jeremiah . . . I am so thankful that God ordained me to be your father. You are the greatest gifts God has ever given your mother and me, and we are so proud of you. I pray that someday you will read this book and it will help you put on the full armor of God and keep up your guard against Satan's attacks. May you become the men God has created you to be and release a tsunami of God's gracious love to a lost world. I love you, boys, and I believe in you and in the call God has on your lives.

To my father . . . Thank you for being the best father a prodigal son could have. You have been my hero since I was a child, but you became Superman for sure when you were diagnosed with cancer in 2010. The way you have faced this terror head-on with a strong faith in God has challenged me to give my trials to the Lord and allow Him to use them for His glory. I am selfishly asking God to give you many more years on this earth not only because of our love for each other but so you that can teach me many more lessons. I love you, Pops, and I look forward to many more rounds of golf together at the lake.

To my mother . . . You were the cornerstone of my crumbling foundation during the self-destructive period of my youth. As I ran from God, you faithfully stood by my side and spent many nights praying for the Lord to keep me safe as I found my way back to Him. You have always encouraged me to believe I could do all things if I would allow God to control my heart. I am who I am today because of your love, and I want you to know how grateful I am to have you as my mom. Never stop praying for me and my family. I love you, Momma!

And finally, to you the reader . . . I pray that this book will challenge you to recognize what you have overlooked, confront what you have kept hidden, and stand up and fight for the abundant life God has for you. As you read this book, ask the Holy Spirit to speak to your heart. My prayer is that by the time you finish reading the book you will be slinging a sledgehammer and tearing down the walls Satan would use to keep you from experiencing the life God wants you enjoy through His Son Jesus. Peace!

CHAPTER 1

LET'S GET IT ON!

A final word: Be strong in the Lord and in his mighty power. Put on all of God's armor so that you will be able to stand firm against all strategies of the devil.
– Ephesians 6:10–11

The Ultimate Fighting Championship (UFC) is America's fastest-growing sport, and John McCarthy is its most famous referee. "Big John," a Los Angeles police officer until his retirement in 2007, has been with the UFC since its beginning in the early 90s. His face is well-known in the mixed martial arts world, but his words are even more recognizable. When two fighters square off for battle, Big John makes his way to the center of the ring, claps his hands, and screams, "Let's get it on!" After hearing those words, there is no doubt in the fighters' minds—they are in a fight.

We begin our journey to break down walls by acknowledging we are in a fight, not for a UFC belt and a six-figure contract but for eternal life itself. It's worth the fight, so let's get it on!

Preparing for Battle

We know from Acts 16:37 and 22:25 that the apostle Paul was a Roman citizen. Born in the Roman province of Cilicia, about the same time as Jesus, Paul would have known the importance of being prepared for battle. In his day Roman gladiators would enter the arena and literally fight to the death as the audience cheered. Paul might have witnessed firsthand these gladiators fighting to survive and to please the crowd's bloodthirsty nature. He might have even watched as they prepared themselves for the fight of their lives with helmets, shields, and weapons of all kinds.

Every spectator of the games would have been aware of the grisly consequences of a gladiator not being prepared for battle. Maybe this is why Paul focuses, in Ephesians 6:10–17, on "putting on the full armor of God"—rather than encouraging folks to grab a swimsuit, umbrella, and tanning lotion and head to the beach. Maybe he wanted the believers in Ephesus to understand the same thing I am pressing hard for as we begin this book: The Christian life is a battle!

Exposing My Own Wall

I am married to a beautiful and talented woman of God. She is an amazing mother and the most faithful wife a man could hope for. But starting in 2009 Amy and I found ourselves, after twenty years of marriage, in the fight of our lives—a fight to protect the covenant we took before God in 1989.

What was the problem? It wasn't love, because we had passionately loved each other for more than twenty years. It wasn't unfaithfulness, because if either of us was in a room with the most attractive and interesting people on the planet, neither of us would give them a second look. It wasn't finances, because the bills were getting paid. The problem was that we were locked into arguing. We were arguing about who would do the dishes. We were arguing about who would do the laundry. We were arguing about the discipline of our children. We were arguing about who took the dogs out last. We were arguing about the culinary choice for supper and whose turn it was to fix it. Our house went from a house of love to a war zone resembling the storming of the beaches of Normandy during World War II.

In 2012 Amy and I came to an agreement that we had to go through counseling to save our marriage and to restore the health of our children, who were obviously being affected. Their personalities were changing, their grades were dropping, and their teachers were informing us that they were becoming more aggressive in class. So we went to our pastor, who referred us to Grace Life International, a counseling ministry in Charlotte, North Carolina.

Our counselor, Ted, was a very loving and compassionate man of God. After two intense sessions of digging up all our family history and background, Ted called us into his office to go over all the results. He looked straight at us and said, "You guys are going to be fine—I can tell that you love each other very much. But I need to see one of you for several sessions, to work on some issues, before I begin to meet with both of you."

Before I could catch myself, I blurted out, "When do you want me to bring her?"

Amy turned to me with a look of shock on her face. And Ted, with a small grin on his face, replied, "It's not her that I need to see."

Ted went on to state that I needed to deal with some issues from my past and that these issues were continuing to affect the decisions I was making. It was hard for me to accept this, yet all the way home Amy reminded me of all the times I had blamed her. It was clear that something needed to be done, because we found ourselves in another screaming match for the rest of the day. My pride had been squashed, my ego decimated, my hero status revoked, but God had a plan—for a wall was about to come down.

I prepared to go to my first session by checking off the items on my man list: 1) Watch *Braveheart*; 2) Purchase next UFC pay-per-view fighting event; 3) Hang out with the homeboys at Wild Wings Bar and Grill; 4) Go hunting for a fresh new kill; 5) Watch *SportsCenter* on ESPN. Now that everything was complete, I felt ready for my first session.

When I walked in, the first thing Ted addressed was the wound I had received in 1985 as a result of my parents going through a separation and divorce. My first response was to defend this wall that had been built in my heart. I lashed out, "That's the past; it's been forgiven; I've moved on. So what's your point?"

Ted looked at me with compassionate eyes, and after a long pause his response to me was nothing less than God's voice from heaven: "Christian, the last time your heart was open your family crushed it, and since that day you have lived your life inflicting wounds on others so you don't have to open your heart again and let them inflict wounds on you. You're always on the offensive, you're always on the attack, which is why you find yourself arguing with your wife, intimidating your children, and severing relationships with close friends."

I will never forget the shame I felt in that moment. As the tears began to fall, I looked at Ted and asked, "How do I fix this? How can I overcome this wall?" I will also never forget what Ted said next: "Flesh can't fix the flesh, Christian. Only God can fix the flesh. You must open your heart and allow the Spirit of God to heal what's been wounded, to restore what's been stolen, and to set free what's been imprisoned."

Once I accepted the truth, I experienced incredible freedom in that moment. Just admitting that a wall existed allowed God to come in and start a path of healing in my life. That wall, which had imprisoned me since 1985, started to crumble!

Amy and I completed our counseling and took the necessary steps to see our marriage restored. Our marriage has never been better! We now pray together as a family every night. We sit down and enjoy supper together as a family, whereas the fighting used to be so fierce we spent little quality time together. Our children are making straight A's again, and a recent report from a teacher confirms that God is moving in our family because their smiles have returned, their shoulders no longer slump, and their aggression has subsided. Isn't it amazing that when we confront our personal walls other people's lives are affected in a positive way as well?

Now that I have opened my closet door for all to see, hopefully you are willing to admit you have a wall that needs to be confronted as well. Maybe it's time to let down your guard and confront what you have been hiding. The devil loves secrets, which is probably why James tells us, in James 5:16, to confess our sins to each other. Now is the time to look deep within yourself, as I did recently, and allow God to break down the wall that you have been holding on to for way too long.

GLADIATOR GEAR

How are you going to do it? By preparing for battle and putting on the full armor of God. In Ephesians 6:10–12 we see that Paul was encouraging us to be prepared, knowing that we are in the fight of our lives. "We are not fighting against flesh-and-blood enemies, but against evil rulers and authorities of the unseen world, against mighty powers in this dark world, and against evil spirits in the heavenly places" (verse 12). Paul starts off this way to give us a firm grasp of what lies ahead of us as Christians, and then he writes of the armor and weapons with which we will fight. Let's take a closer look at this armor Paul writes about in Ephesians 6:13–17 so that we can become familiar with what protects us in times of battle.

THE BELT OF TRUTH

The first item in our arsenal is found in verse 14: "Stand your ground, putting on the belt of truth." Of all the things Paul could have chosen to start with in regard to slaying the enemy, why would he choose "the belt of truth"? Let's not forget our previous observation about Paul being a Roman citizen who knew the ways of the gladiators and understood that after a warrior's armor was assembled and fitted in place it was all connected and held together by the belt. If the belt became unconnected, the armor would fall and the gladiator or soldier was left exposed—reminding me of a clip I saw on *America's Funniest Home Videos* of an older gentleman dancing at a wedding reception when his belt came undone and his pants dropped to the floor.

Why is truth so important when it comes to breaking down walls? Jesus is the truth; and as He stated in John 8:32, it is His truth that will set us free. This is so critical in a world that continues to pull further and further away from the teachings of Christ. Many today are pulling away from God's Word and elevating their personal views above uncompromised truth. It's no wonder that so many walls stand in the world today, even in the church. Because people have walked away from the truth, their belt has come unlatched and their pants are around their feet. To see Grandpa exposed on the dance floor might be funny, but for a gladiator or Roman soldier to lose his belt in battle meant certain death. And in my opinion, it's that serious for you and me as well.

The Body Armor of Righteousness

The second item is also mentioned in verse 14: "Stand your ground, putting on the belt of truth and the body armor of God's righteousness." The body armor, commonly referred to as a breast-plate, was a sleeveless piece of leather that completely covered a soldier's torso, protecting his heart and other vital organs. This shows us how seriously Paul took living a life of righteousness. He knew that a Christian who lived a righteous life would be protected and strong when the enemy came to attack, just as he knew how vulnerable a follower of Christ would be if he or she did not practice holy living.

When I spoke in Savannah, Georgia several years ago, my boys and I got to spend a day at nearby Fort Stewart, hanging out with some of America's finest. We were escorted around the base by the sergeant major, who had seen a lot of action during two tours of duty in the Middle East. When he asked if my boys would like to be junior troopers for the day and see the base in style, we readily agreed—though I have to admit I was more excited than they were as we jumped in and out of helicopters and tanks. During our tour I noticed that everywhere we went men stood at attention and gave the sergeant major a quick, "Yes, sir!" Men lounging on top of tanks jumped down and gave a quick salute, soldiers talking outside of buildings formed straight lines, and everyone listened and obeyed his voice with the utmost respect. I discovered that the sergeant major was always the first one into battle, and thus had earned his comrades' respect.

Has Jesus' sacrifice not earned your respect? Have enough people not been hurt by our disobedience? Just as a Roman soldier was exposed when one piece of his armor was missing, so we as Christians are exposed when our hearts are given over to unrighteousness. Satan got to Adam and Eve when their guard was down, when their armor was exposed, when their hearts were left unguarded. He was successful because of their unrighteous choice, and the world has suffered ever since.

THE SHOES OF PEACE

The third item is found in verse 15: "For shoes, put on the peace that comes from the Good News so that you will be fully prepared." You might be wondering what the big deal is about showing up to fight with a pair of shoes. I hear you, but stick with me because each piece is very important when it comes to breaking down walls and winning the victory. Paul knew that the Roman soldiers wore boots with nails in them, which helped them not to slip while they were fighting. When people slip and fall they usually recover quickly, but to fall in battle was no laughing matter—it was a death sentence. God wants us, as Christians, to have peace from the gospel so that we can stand firm when the attack of the enemy comes our way.

Many Christians today can't begin to defend why they are a believer, much less lead someone else to Christ. Being unsure of your faith and unable to defend your beliefs puts you on a very slippery slope. You need to know the truth and stand firm in it. There is nothing more peaceful and beautiful than a believer who knows why he or she has been set free by the truth, is clothed in God's righteousness, and is standing firm on the Good News.

THE SHIELD OF FAITH

The fourth item is in verse 16: "In addition to all of these, hold up the shield of faith to stop the fiery arrows of the devil." Recently I watched a TV show on the History network with my son Malachi about the battle of three hundred Spartan warriors who fought against King Xerxes and the Persians. According to tradition, three hundred Spartan soldiers held off a force some believe to have been in the hundreds of thousands. The key was their shields: They formed a wall of protection with their shields, and these men would dig in and hold off the attack while comrades from behind would strike with their long spears. According to historical accounts of the Battle of Thermopylae, three hundred Spartans were able to kill thousands upon thousands of Persians. Still today, battle strategists will refer to this battle in warning those about to fight how dangerous and successful a warrior is when he is defending his family and home soil.

The Roman soldiers also used their shield in an effective way. Their shields, which covered their entire bodies, were dipped in an oil that would extinguish the fiery arrows of the enemy. Paul said to "hold up the shield of faith to stop the fiery arrows of the devil," because a warrior with a strong shield will find victory on his side more times than not. I tell people all the time that faith is something the devil can't stop, and when your faith is strong you are a dangerous weapon for the kingdom of God.

Satan will fight hard to stop you from tearing down walls, using everything in his arsenal to keep you separated from God and unable to see who God has created you to be. Faith is what you will need when the enemy's fiery arrows are coming your way. Faith is what you will need when this book gets tough and you want to lay it down.

THE HELMET OF SALVATION

The fifth item in the armor of God is found in verse 17: "Put on salvation as your helmet." I'm sure you would agree that having your head exposed in battle would be a big mistake, but you might be wondering what the connection is between protecting your head and salvation. To answer this, I need to share a bit of my testimony.

The 1980s might have been good to heavy-metal bands, love songs, big hair, *Star Wars*, and tight-fitting jeans, but they weren't good to one lost teenager in Kannapolis, North Carolina. I went from being a popular athlete and straight-A student to being a young man who was struggling to stay alive. The downhill slide started when my parents went through a nasty divorce. Eventually I sank into rebellion, drinking, doing drugs, fighting, and becoming homeless in Myrtle Beach, South Carolina. After spending a night in the hospital because of drugs, I decided to go back home. I got a job working with my dad at Charlotte Honda, putting bikes together; and the weekends were filled with racing.

One night I decided to go to a party with the guys from the shop, which usually led to a night I could barely remember the next day. This night would be different, however, and in fact would change my life forever. After not drinking or doing any drugs, which was highly unusual, I left the party about 3 a.m. But my bike ran out of gas on the highway right outside the city limits. After thumbing for a ride for thirty minutes, a taxi driver picked me up, took me to get some gas, and brought me back to my bike—which cost me all the money I had in my wallet. I put gas in the bike and waved goodbye to the taxi driver, only to realize I had left my keys in the cab and was still stuck on the highway far from home in the early morning hours.

After sitting there for a while contemplating my situation, life, and future, I cried out to a God I wasn't sure existed and asked for forgiveness from a Savior I wasn't sure loved me. I asked God to reveal His love to me, and I vowed that if He did I would never question or deny His existence again. I cried out for God's grace for a life filled with drugs, alcohol, sex, pornography, lies, and deception; and I asked God to reveal that grace through the message of love.

As soon as I prayed that prayer, I opened my eyes to see a car pulled off to the side of the road as if it appeared out of nowhere. I walked up to the car and looked inside after the driver rolled down the window. I noticed a Bible on the passenger seat. I felt the Holy Spirit all around me as God's plan was starting to be revealed to my unbelieving mind for the first time. I looked at the driver, a large black man, and heard him speak these life-giving words to me: "The Lord told me to pick you up and tell you He loves you tonight."

At 4 a.m., on the side of a highway outside Charlotte, North Carolina, salvation came to my heart. And this faith has helped me extinguish all the fiery arrows of the enemy.

In regard to salvation being our helmet and protecting a vital part of our body, let me ask you if you see the power and importance of our salvation. Paul talked quite often about his conversion and the grace he received that day on the road to Damascus. Why? Because there is a lot of power in a Jesus story. Do you think the young boy mentioned in John 6:9 ever stopped talking about the day this man named Jesus took his five loaves and two fish and fed five thousand people? Do you think the paralyzed man portrayed in Luke 5:17–26 ever stopped praising God after being healed of his affliction? Do you think the deaf and mute man depicted in Mark 7:31–35 ever stopped telling others of his healing after Jesus restored his hearing and speech? And do you think the woman about to be stoned, as recounted in John 8, ever stopped sharing the story of how her new hero Jesus spared her from torture and death at the hands of the Pharisees' stones?

If your answer to these questions is no, then I think you understand the importance of having salvation as a helmet. If there is one thing science can't explain, atheists can't defeat, and other religions don't understand, it's your Jesus story! Wear it today and every day as a helmet, and never forget the depths from which you have been saved. Wear your helmet with pride and power wherever you go, because I promise that you will need to remember it. While the battle is raging, you will need to protect yourself with it; and while confronting walls in the process of reading this book, you will need to rely on it.

THE SWORD OF THE SPIRIT

At last we come to the one item in the armor of God that is actually a weapon: "And take the sword of the Spirit, which is the word of God" (verse 17). If you're a man, you're probably thinking, *Yeah, baby, I finally get a sword—time to inflict some wounds!* Well, let's not forget Ephesians 6:11, where we are encouraged to "stand firm against all strategies of the devil," which is more of a defensive posture than an offensive one. So don't go looking for a fight with the enemy, because that's when we get ahead of God's plan and fall into unknown traps.

Don't worry, those of you who have a warrior spirit, the devil will bring you all you want and then some. It's important, however, to understand why Paul would encourage us to stand firm with the word of God. The apostle John began his gospel by declaring, "In the beginning the Word already existed. The Word was with God, and the Word was God" (John 1:1). John was connecting this verse with Genesis 1:1, which says, "In the beginning God created the heavens and the earth." John was letting his readers know that before the world was created, before particles and dust were in space, Jesus was with God. This is good to know, because if the sword we hold was there when the universe was created, there when all creation was birthed, there when God breathed life into man, and there before Satan tempted Adam and Eve, then how could anything in this world come against us?

When we take the Word of God into our hearts, we literally have within us something as old and powerful as time and creation itself. Way too many Christians I meet today are not taking in the Word of God, but rather leave it shut up in a drawer of their homes much like Gideon Bibles stay shut up in the drawers of hotel rooms across America.

John also points out that "the word *was* God," which leaves no room for error when it comes to understanding that there is only one way to heaven—and it is through a relationship with the Word (Jesus Christ). Many religions, and even some Christian denominations, say there are many different ways to heaven that can be obtained through many different paths of travel in life's journey. If we truly know this Word, then we understand that Jesus didn't mince words when He said, in John 10:9, "I am the gate. Those who come in through me will be saved." Or again, in John 14:6, "I am the way, the truth, and the life. No one can come to the Father except through me." This is so important, because if we try to bring down walls or fight by the power of any other name than Jesus, then we will fail and walls will still be left standing.

So it all begins and ends with Christ. Do you truly know the Word? Do you have a relationship with Jesus Christ? Are you drinking from His fountain of living water, or from the world's well that will eventually leave you thirsty again? Does the Word of God live within you? It's a game changer for sure, and if you will embrace this Word and the armor of God by which Paul tells us we should fight, then I believe you are ready for battle.

Don't Lose Focus

So if you know there is a wall in your life and you are ready to confront it, *don't lose focus*! Let me illustrate this point with a story. A few years ago I planned a special date for my wife's birthday. We would begin our night with fine dining at the Passion8 Bistro, one of the finest restaurants in Charlotte, and then head to a special event at the Cricket Arena. After eating at one of her favorite restaurants, Amy was shocked when I said we had somewhere else to go. "There's more?" she asked. "Oh yeah, baby, the best is yet to come."

When we arrived at the Cricket Arena the parking lot was completely full and police were everywhere. We had never seen such a big crowd for an event there. When Amy walked in and saw the UFC "Octagon" in the center of the arena and thousands of fans screaming at the top of their lungs, she said, "Are you kidding me?! Is this my birthday or yours?!" I wasn't offended at all, and was willing to go through a little abuse to see my first live UFC event.

The energy of the crowd that night was amazing, the fights were exciting, and the light show and all the professionalism that goes into a UFC event were very entertaining. One of the highlights of the night was a heavyweight fight featuring Roy "Big Country" Nelson and Stefan "The Skyscraper" Struve. As they entered the ring, Amy immediately picked The Skyscraper to dominate the fight. At 6'11" and 261 pounds, Struve was one lean and mean physical specimen. Nelson, on the other hand, was overweight and bragged that his regular training routine included eating at Burger King. Even though Amy determined it wouldn't be much of a match, I wasn't buying it. I had seen Nelson fight in past UFC events, so I knew that even though his belly was big, his right hand was vicious.

The fighters were introduced and the referee made his way to the center of the ring. Just as he was about to start the fight, the power went out in the arena. Fans screamed as red floodlights flashed on and police rushed in. Chaos seemed to be breaking out, and I started getting nervous about how I was going to get Amy out of there if a mob mentality took over. As I was about to lead us toward the exit, I noticed that Dana White, the president of the UFC, had made his way to the back of the arena and was pacing back and forth while frantically waving his hands in the air. This was a live event on the Spike TV network, so the stakes were high.

The outside of the building and the upper seats were dark, but the floodlights had the center of the arena and the ring lit up. I looked at the two fighters in the ring and noticed something strange. The Skyscraper, Struve, had turned his back on his opponent; with his arms draped over the top of the ring, he was relaxing while talking to his coach. Big Country, however, never took his eyes off his opponent, and was pacing back and forth with an intense look on his face. He didn't talk to his coach, he didn't look at the fans—he kept his eyes and focus on his opponent.

The power was soon restored, the referee made his way back to the center of the ring, and the fight began. Within thirty-nine seconds Nelson knocked out Struve, which was the first time The Skyscraper had ever tasted the canvas. Big Country began to celebrate with his normal routine of jumping on top of the Octagon fence and rubbing his big belly with one hand while pointing at the crowd and thanking them with the other. Amy screamed, "I never thought he would win." But my response was, "Only one guy came to fight tonight."

Are you focused and ready to keep your eyes fixed on the prize? Are you ready to see some walls fall down? Even when chaos is breaking out around you and you feel like the power connection is lost, you can still have the victory!

So let us begin our journey, remembering the words of Christian author C. S. Lewis, "God, who foresaw your tribulation, has specially armed you to go through it, not without pain but without stain."

Let's get it on!

I Love You More

After breakfast Jesus asked Simon
Peter, "Simon son of John, do you
love me more than these?"
"Yes, Lord," Peter replied, "you
know I love you."

— John 21:15

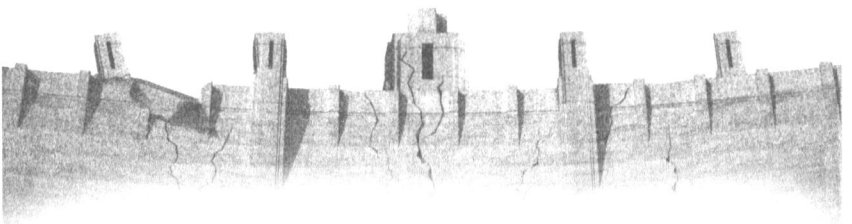

CHAPTER 2

A WALL OF SELF

Even on my best days I have the capability to be a monster. The chorus from the song "Monster," by the Christian rock band Skillet, describes me well at times:

> I feel it deep within, it's just beneath the skin
> I must confess that I feel like a monster
> I hate what I've become, the nightmare's just begun
> I must confess that I feel like a monster

Maybe you're different than me and don't feel this way. Maybe you have your life together and never transform from being a faithful tither, Sunday school attender, Christian radio listener, and Bible scholar to being a Freddy Krueger-esque nightmare. Good for you—Head to the next chapter! Or better yet, maybe you should get a refund on this book!

Personally, I have to admit that when someone flips me the bird in traffic, my first instinct isn't to wave and invite them to church. When a provocatively dressed, beautiful woman walks by, my reaction isn't always to look away. When my wife and I have conflict, the arguments don't always end with a hug and a kiss and a prayer session. When I find out that someone said something negative about me behind my back, I don't always cry out, "Father, forgive them; for they know not what they do."

I could go on and on, but I'll bet you not only get my point but realize that you have the ability to be a monster at times too. All of these situations have to do with the desire to please self, and all of them lead to a wall of self. So how do we defeat and bring down this wall? What it comes down to is us saying the same thing Peter said on one important occasion when Jesus confronted him with his wall of self: "Yes, Lord, I love You."

THE OLDEST TRICK IN THE BOOK

The wall of self, which is as old as time itself, is most likely the most difficult of all walls to overcome. We can trace its origin back to Isaiah 14, which alludes to the fall of Satan. "How you are fallen from heaven, O shining star, son of the morning! You have been thrown down to the earth, you who destroyed the nations of the world" (Isaiah 14:12).

This is a fitting fate for the presence of pure evil and darkness in the universe—but what would deserve such a penalty? The next few verses reveal the answer: "For you said to yourself, 'I will ascend to heaven and set my throne above God's stars. I will preside on the mountain of the gods far away in the north. I will climb to the highest heaven and be like the Most High'" (Isaiah 14:13–14).

I don't know if you caught it, but this has self written all over it. Satan wanted to do things *his* way. He wanted to make his own decisions. He wanted to control his own destiny. He wanted to rule over others and have them submit to his will. He didn't just want to bend the rules, he wanted to break them. Does any of this sound familiar? It should, because this is the main temptation Satan uses on people today. He's the second-most powerful force in the universe, but he's not very creative. He sticks to what works: the lure of the flesh and self.

Adam and Eve experienced this in the Garden of Eden.

> The serpent was the shrewdest of all the wild animals the Lord God had made. One day he asked the woman, "Did God really say you must not eat the fruit from any of the trees in the garden?"
>
> "Of course we may eat fruit from the trees in the garden," the woman replied. "It's only the fruit from the tree in the middle of the garden that we are not allowed to eat. God said, 'You must not eat it or even touch it; if you do, you will die.'"
>
> "You won't die!" the serpent replied to the woman. "God knows that your eyes will be opened as soon as you eat it, and you will be like God, knowing both good and evil."
>
> The woman was convinced. She saw that the tree was beautiful and its fruit looked delicious, and she wanted the wisdom it would give her. So she took some of the fruit and ate it. Then she gave some to her husband, who was with her, and he ate it, too. – Genesis 3:1–6

Notice the serpent's attack—once again it has self written all over it. Adam and Eve had everything, but Satan talked them into wanting more.

Job knew a little something about being attacked as well.

> One day the members of the heavenly court came to present themselves before the LORD, and the Accuser, Satan, came with them. "Where have you come from?" the LORD asked Satan.
>
> Satan answered the LORD, "I have been patrolling the earth, watching everything that's going on."
>
> Then the LORD asked Satan, "Have you noticed my servant Job? He is the finest man in all the earth. He is blameless—a man of complete integrity. He fears God and stays away from evil."
>
> Satan replied to the LORD, "Yes, but Job has good reason to fear God. You have always put a wall of protection around him and his home and his property. You have made him prosper in everything he does. Look how rich he is! But reach out and take away everything he has, and he will surely curse you to your face!"
>
> "All right, you may test him," the LORD said to Satan. "Do whatever you want with everything he possesses, but don't harm him physically." So Satan left the LORD's presence. – Job 1:6–12

Notice how Satan asked God to lift His protection and allow everything Job had to be taken away from him. Satan assumed that Job struggled with self, and he attacked him where he felt it would hurt the most.

Jesus Himself was also tempted by Satan.

Then Jesus was led by the Spirit into the wilderness to be tempted there by the devil. For forty days and forty nights he fasted and became very hungry.

During that time the devil came and said to him, "If you are the Son of God, tell these stones to become loaves of bread."

But Jesus told him, "No! The Scriptures say, 'People do not live by bread alone, but by every word that comes from the mouth of God.'"

Then the devil took him to the holy city, Jerusalem, to the highest point of the Temple, and said, "If you are the Son of God, jump off! For the Scriptures say, 'He will order his angels to protect you. And they will hold you up with their hands so you won't even hurt your foot on a stone.'"

Jesus responded, "The Scriptures also say, 'You must not test the LORD your God.'"

Next the devil took him to the peak of a very high mountain and showed him all the kingdoms of the world and their glory. "I will give it all to you," he said, "if you will kneel down and worship me."

"Get out of here, Satan," Jesus told him. "For the Scriptures say, 'You must worship the LORD your God and serve only him.'"

Then the devil went away, and angels came and took care of Jesus. – Matthew 4:1–11

Satan unleashed three attacks on the Son of God, but with no success. First, after Jesus had gone without food for forty days, Satan offered Him some bread. The second temptation was intended to appeal to Jesus' pride, as the devil encouraged Jesus to show off His superpower status. And the third contest was for no less than control of the entire world. Satan tried to get the Savior to bow down to him, because he knew that if he was successful grace would be out of the picture—and you and I would be done for!

SELF-CENTERED SIMON

A lot is riding on the outcome of whether or not we choose to tear down the wall of self. We can see this in the example of Simon Peter.

One time Peter was following Jesus admirably by literally walking on water. But then he had a momentary loss of faith: "When he saw the strong wind and the waves, he was terrified and began to sink. 'Save me, Lord!' he shouted" (Matthew 14:30).

When Jesus began preparing His disciples for the reality of His coming suffering and death, Peter took Jesus aside and reprimanded him for saying such things. Jesus then spoke very sternly to Peter in return: "Get away from me, Satan! You are seeing things merely from a human point of view, not from God's" (Mark 8:33). Not only did Jesus rebuke Peter's wall of self, He clearly identified it as a satanic attack upon His own life.

When Jesus approached Peter with a water basin and a towel, Peter's barrier of self rose up again: "No," Peter protested, "you will never ever wash my feet!" (John 13:8).

At the end of every road and at the finish of every race, we need to realize that we weren't traveling or competing alone. Others are always impacted by our choices, and those choices can make or break people's personal success and walk with Christ. After Jesus' death and resurrection, John 21 recounts how Peter told six other disciples that he was going fishing, and they all said, "We'll come, too." Following Peter in his poor choice, they went out in the boat but didn't catch a single fish all night. They decided to do what felt natural and comfortable, rather than following the call to reach the world with the message of Jesus. Have you been there? I know I have.

SELF-CENTERED ME

I went to Southern Wesleyan University, located in the small town of Central, South Carolina, not only to get an education but also to play baseball. Since I got married at the young age of twenty, I didn't live in the dorms with all the other athletes. My new wife and I lived in a small house off-campus. I have to admit that I was a young Christian trying to figure out the whole married thing, which is very difficult when you're a freshman in college. At first I didn't take my studies seriously at all. God had called me to study His Word and to become a preacher and teacher of His truth, but instead I focused all my attention on baseball and hanging out with the guys.

In fact, my routine wasn't the least bit God-inspiring. I went to class in the morning, and then after grabbing some lunch at the cafeteria I headed straight to the baseball field for practice until around 5:30. Then I would go to the gym and work out with the team before heading to downtown Clemson to eat supper and hang out all evening with the guys. I would come home around midnight and do just enough schoolwork to get by and then get a couple hours of sleep.

The only problem was that Amy was by herself at home every night: eating supper alone, washing the dishes and the laundry, cleaning the house, and falling asleep while waiting for her husband to come home. I'm embarrassed to admit it, but Amy would tell you that she almost divorced me during that first year in college and went back home to Kannapolis to live with her parents.

In the midst of all this baseball playing and partying, I took a test that turned out to be one of the best things that has ever happened in my life. This test revealed that I had a reading disorder—requiring me, therefore, to receive tutoring in the library every Tuesday and Thursday. I was embarrassed to tell anybody on the baseball team that I couldn't read, and I even refused to share the news with Amy. To keep my baseball scholarship, however, I had to maintain a certain grade point average; so I had no choice but to attend.

When the day came for me to go to the library, I remember sneaking in a side door and hurrying down the hallway so no one from the baseball team would see me. When I came to the door of the room, I peeked in, and to my amazement half the baseball team was inside! I walked in with a big smile on my face and said, "What's up, Macy?" "What's up, Bay?" "What's up, Atkins?" And they cheered as I walked in, saying things like "What's up, Number 21?" and "Come on in, baby—We're gonna learn how to read!"

I felt right at home, now, with all my teammates sharing my reading disability. I even said, "Who's teaching this class? Who would dare to try to come in and control a room full of jocks? This is our class, baby! Whoever's teaching this class better get ready to earn their paycheck!"

When our arrogance was at its peak, in walked an elderly woman with horn-rimmed glasses and an afghan wrapped around her shoulders, her hair graying from years of life and stress. She sat down, holding something in her hand that I couldn't make out. I will never forget the first words that came out of Mrs. Freeze's mouth: "Boys, God has a plan for your life, and being illiterate is not one of them."

What?! Did this old woman just call us stupid? But you could have heard a pin drop as she explained to us that we wouldn't be following normal procedures. Mrs. Freeze was holding a Bible, which she lifted up as she told us we would be reading God's Word every Tuesday and Thursday. By getting into the Word of God, we would become the men He created us to be. So twice a week I went to that room in the basement of the library, along with half our baseball team, and started to read and seriously study the Bible for the first time in my life.

A LIFE-CHANGING REMEDIAL LESSON

I also fell in love with our teacher, who lived just across the street from the campus. From time to time I would see Mrs. Freeze clipping a red rosebush in front of her house and stop and talk with her. Every day in her presence, every day in the Word of God, I could feel myself becoming less self-focused. But a wall still existed, because my wife was still at home alone. God wasn't going to let me off the hook, though. He was about to use this teacher's life and a story she would share with us to change my life forever.

We knew Mrs. Freeze was single, so one day during class we started joking with her about setting her up on a blind date with a retired professor and paying for the evening's entertainment. Several ballplayers whistled, while others clapped. Our teacher stood and said she appreciated the gesture but thought we should hear a story first.

Mrs. Freeze told us that she had been married to an amazing man for many years. He was a faithful husband who was completely committed to God in all that he did. He served and loved others, and his desire to make a difference in the world could be seen by all. He was never too busy to take sunset walks hand-in-hand with his bride and tell her she was the most amazing gift God could have ever given him. He was ready and willing to volunteer at their church when there was a need. And as a professor in the South in the 1960s, when racism was rampant, Dr. Freeze demonstrated his warrior spirit by standing alone and announcing he would resign if the university voted to stay segregated. Because of his bold commitment, Southern Wesleyan University became the first college in South Carolina to be willing to enroll a black student.

Several months earlier I had heard a radio interview with Billy Graham's wife. When asked if she ever wished she had married someone else in light of the fact that her husband traveled around the world and she had to raise their children virtually by herself, Ruth Graham paused and then said, "Five minutes with Billy Graham is like a lifetime with any other man."

I was reminded of that statement as I listened to Mrs. Freeze go on for nearly ten minutes about her love and admiration for her husband. I was getting excited about the opportunity to meet this man when she informed us that not long before he had died of cancer. She described how he suffered and how difficult it was to watch the love of her life slip away.

Near the end he was confined to bed and slept most of the time, which was OK with Mrs. Freeze since he was in severe pain when he was awake. One day she went to get him pain medication because he was about to run out and she wanted to keep him as comfortable as she could. Much to her surprise, she came home to find a freshly planted rosebush beside the driveway where she had parked for years. Mrs. Freeze shared how she had always loved roses, especially red ones. She loved the way they looked, the way they smelled, and the way their color could brighten the gloomiest of days.

When Mrs. Freeze got out of the car to touch and smell the roses, she noticed a trail of mud leading from the bush to the house. She followed the mud path into the kitchen, and then into the dining room, and then down the hallway toward the bedroom. Entering the bedroom, she was shocked to find her husband—covered with mud—collapsed on the floor. She imme-diately cleaned him up, helped him back to bed, and gave him his pain medication. Then it struck her that her husband, who was dying of cancer, had laid in the mud to plant her a rosebush.

Dr. Freeze died not long after that, but the rosebush was still there. As I mentioned earlier, I had seen Mrs. Freeze trimming it. With tears in her eyes, Mrs. Freeze talked about her husband's devotion to the Lord and how his greatest desire was to bring joy to other people.

MY WALL CRUMBLES

Most of us went from being big, strong athletes to weeping uncon-trollably. I have no idea why the other ballplayers were crying, but the reality came crashing down on me that I was living a life con-cerned and consumed with self. Knowing that I was about to flunk out of college and to become divorced, I look back and realize how that story saved my marriage and my ministry calling. Amy didn't know at the time why the change happened, but she would tell you today that I became a new man during my freshman year in college. I started to stay at home more and help her with the household chores, but more importantly I spent quality time with Amy and got to know her on a personal level.

Rather than merely playing baseball, I became more concerned with ministry than baseball. When I was inducted into Southern Wesleyan University's baseball hall of fame several years ago, my coach didn't talk about the home run record I broke or any other athletic accomplishments. Instead, he talked about the Bible study I started and the difference I made in the dugout. He talked about my love for my teammates and how I wanted them to know they were loved by God and that He had a purpose for their lives. The home runs and RBIs were nice, but as I sat there that night I realized that the things I accomplish for Christ will always be more wonderful than the things I accomplish for myself.

That day in the library, the testimony of a man from the grave taught me to say, "Yes, Lord, I love You." I learned to love my wife more than hanging out with the guys in downtown Clemson. I learned to study God's Word and appreciate my calling rather than wasting opportunities in the campus game room. I learned to take advantage of being on a baseball team full of lost people instead of trying to be a superstar. And still today I am faced with the daily struggle of saying no to self and declaring with integrity to Christ, "I love You."

In John 21:15, Jesus asked Peter, "Simon son of John, do you love me more than these?" We can't tell if Jesus meant "Do you love Me more than you love these men?" or "Do you love Me more than these men love Me?" or "Do you love Me more than you love these things (i.e., the equipment related to fishing)?" Nevertheless, as Peter realized that Jesus was trying to cleanse him of self and release him to serve—even unto death—he was able to respond sincerely, "Yes, Lord, I love You—I love You more." And the book of Acts is filled with Peter's success story.

What will your success story be? Are you ready to answer, "Yes, Lord, I love You—I love You more"? Are you ready to let your wall of self be torn down?

If your answer is yes, then I believe you can accomplish this by taking your eyes off of yourself and keeping them on Jesus. Keeping his eyes on Jesus was enough to elevate Peter to defy the law of gravity and walk on water, and I believe it will certainly be enough to elevate you to victory in conquering your wall.

Have you ever heard of the old acronym for joy? True joy is achieved by keeping

- **J**esus first
- **O**thers second, and
- **Y**ourself last

It sounds simple enough, but I assure you that although taking the focus off of yourself for the greater good of others will be the most difficult thing you will ever do, it is definitely a battle worth fighting—and in the end it will bring about the greater blessing.

Since the day I heard Mrs. Freeze talk about her husband, I have tried to live my life putting others before myself. And I can say with integrity today that being set free from me has been the best thing that has ever happened in my life. Since that day I have also lived by this conviction: If a man will lay in the mud to plant a rosebush for his wife just days before his death, then I have no excuses.

I'm Worth Dying For

Now, most people would not be
willing to die for an upright person,
though someone might perhaps be
willing to die for a person who is
especially good. But God showed his
great love for us by sending Christ to
die for us while we were still sinners.

– Romans 5:7–8

CHAPTER 3

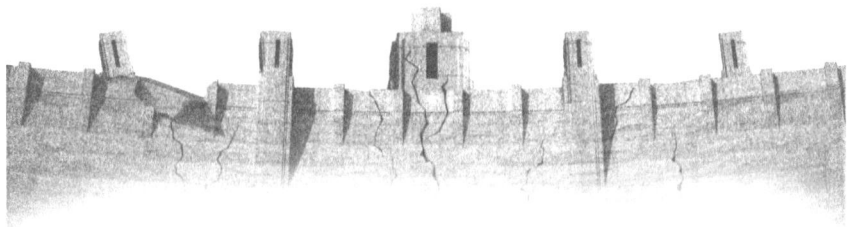

A WALL OF INSECURITY

Years ago when my wife and I lived in the small town of Central, South Carolina, I took a job as a public school substitute teacher while I finished up my last few credit hours of college. One time I got a call from the assistant principal asking me to take over an English class the next day, in which the lesson would be on poetry. I was reluctant, since not too many 6'1", 230-pound athletes are into that kind of thing; but I agreed to take the class because our first son, Malachi, had just been born and I needed the seventy-five dollars.

We read over many different works that day, including poems written by Walt Whitman and Mark Twain, but it was a poem penned by a very lonely and troubled Edgar Allan Poe that grabbed my heart.

A Dream Within a Dream

Take this kiss upon the brow!
And, in parting from you now,
Thus much let me avow—
You are not wrong, who deem
That my days have been a dream;
Yet if hope has flown away
In a night, or in a day,
In a vision, or in none,
Is it therefore the less *gone*?
All that we see or seem
Is but a dream within a dream.

I stand amid the roar
Of a surf-tormented shore,
And I hold within my hand
Grains of a golden sand—
How few! yet how they creep
Through my fingers to the deep,
While I weep—while I weep!
Oh God! Can I not grasp
Them tighter with my clasp?
Oh God! Can I not save
One from the pitiless wave?
Is *all* that we see or seem
But a dream within a dream?

I felt such a heavy weight of sorrow when I read that poem.
It impacted me so much, in fact, that I memorized it, and I still
remember it to this day. This poem represents many Christians

I meet who are living in life's pain and hurt. As you read these words right now, could you say—along with Edgar Allan Poe—that you have had days when you felt hope had flown away, days when you were standing on the surf-tormented shore crying out to God for help?

In an effort to drown out his pain and loneliness near the end of his life, Mr. Poe turned to alcohol. If he had realized he was loved and his life had value, I believe he would have written a psalm of praise instead of a cry for help in the midst of great sorrow. How different do you think Edgar Allan Poe's life would have been if he had realized he was worth dying for? How different would your life be if you truly believed you were worth dying for? "God showed his great love for us," the apostle Paul declared, "by sending Christ to die for us while we were still sinners" (Romans 5:7–8).

Most people I meet won't focus on tearing down walls or opening the closet door to their heart because they fear the consequence of what will be revealed. They fear what others will think and, ultimately, what others will say.

THREE SAD STORIES

Years ago I heard about a tragic incident that took place in my home state of North Carolina. A teenage girl was found dead on the railroad tracks, and amid the horror of the scene was a bewildered police department trying to discover what had happened to her. Did she commit suicide? Was she addicted to drugs and passed out on the tracks? Did someone hate her enough to take her life? All the options were put to rest when they discovered her jacket near the scene and found in her pocket a note she had written. Upon reading the note, the police realized this girl was bullied, rejected, made fun of, and gossiped about—until she finally decided to walk down the tracks that fateful night and wait for a train to come along and end her life.

I wonder if this girl would have taken her life if she really understood and grasped the depth of John 3:16–17:

> For God loved the world so much that he gave his one and only Son, so that everyone who believes in him will not perish but have eternal life. God sent his Son into the world not to judge the world, but to save the world through him.

Several years ago a buddy from my high school football team found me online and asked if I would give him a call. In his message he mentioned that he had gotten himself into a little trouble on Facebook and needed to talk. I immediately responded and asked him to give me a call when I got home from traveling, so that we could get together for lunch and talk. Then I got busy while I was out on the road speaking, and I didn't receive a call from my friend when I got home. And I'm sorry to admit that I didn't think to contact him.

Several months later I saw a Facebook post from another old high school friend regarding my other friend's funeral arrangements. Immediately remembering that we were supposed to get together, I screamed out "No!" Right away I contacted a mutual friend, who informed me that our friend had committed suicide. His wife had discovered him hanging in their closet while she was getting ready for her day.

I haven't shared this story much because of the heavy weight of regret I feel in my heart. I will never forget attending the visitation and shaking hands with my old buddy's two sons and looking into their eyes full of loss. They were preparing to go to college and play football, but their dad wouldn't be in the stands watching them compete as collegiate athletes—making their first tackle or catch. He wouldn't see them graduate and become the husbands and fathers he always hoped they would be.

Neither will I ever forget watching his nine-year-old daughter crawl up in the casket and hug her daddy as tears streamed down her face. He wouldn't be there to take pictures of his little girl in her first prom dress. He wouldn't be there to watch her fall in love and then walk her down the isle of the church to give her away to the man of her dreams.

I wonder what his life would have been like if I would have had the chance to sit down and listen to him share about the shortcomings he was dealing with and then share with him Ephesians 1:4–5 and Ephesians 2:4–5:

> Even before he made the world, God loved us and chose us in Christ to be holy and without fault in his eyes. God decided in advance to adopt us into his own family by bringing us to himself through Jesus Christ.

> But God is so rich in mercy, and he loved us so much, that even though we were dead because of our sins, he gave us life when he raised Christ from the dead.

For many years I was a traveling evangelist and didn't have an office in a church. Instead, I kept my morning "office hours" at Panera Bread and my afternoon hours at Wild Wings Bar and Grill. I have met many interesting people and had some great conversations about Christ, but it's the conversations I *haven't* had that bother me the most.

Several years ago, day after day I saw a man sitting at the bar drinking and looking very sad. Many of the people I meet at the restaurant open up and share their hearts, which I love. Others aren't willing to open up, and this man was definitely putting out those kind of signals. I asked the bartender, whom I had built a relationship with, to tell me his story. She told me something I wasn't expecting to hear: The man was dying of cancer, and—sitting in the same seat and drinking the same drink—he came to the bar to drink his pain away every day.

When I asked her if she thought he would be open to conversation, she emphatically said no. He had made it clear that he wasn't willing to share his story or talk with anyone about his current situation. I decided to leave him alone and to pray for a future opportunity to share the gospel with him. As I watched him sitting in the same chair with the same look of sorrow and loneliness on his face day after day, I was eerily reminded of Edgar Allan Poe's poem of sadness as he screamed out to God for more in life:

> I stand amid the roar
> Of a surf-tormented shore,
> And I hold within my hand
> Grains of a golden sand—
> How few! yet how they creep
> Through my fingers to the deep,
> While I weep—while I weep!

Much like Poe, this man had decided to find seclusion and waste away in sorrow and drink. It broke my heart, at times bringing me to tears. I longed for him to open up and let God soften his heart, but that day never came. One day I noticed that he wasn't in his seat, and he has never been there since.

What would cause a man to shut down like that? What would cause a teenage girl to walk into an oncoming train? What would cause a husband and father-of-three to hang himself in his closet? Some thick and powerful walls. And surely those walls include insecurity—not understanding who and what a person can be in Christ.

I'm sure these stories would have had a different ending if these three people had embraced God's intent for them as expressed in Paul's prayer for the believers in Ephesus:

> I pray that from his glorious, unlimited resources he will empower you with inner strength through his Spirit. Then Christ will make his home in your hearts as you trust in him. Your roots will grow down into God's love and keep you strong. And may you have the power to understand, as all God's people should, how wide, how long, how high, and how deep his love is. – Ephesians 3:16–18

AMAZING BENEFITS

Something amazing always happens when walls fall down, when insecurities are conquered by true love, and when grace sets people free. Those who allow God to tear down their walls of insecurity so that they can see themselves as God sees them acquire some serious benefits.

Let's look at what God's Word, in Romans 5:1–2, says about some of those benefits:

> Therefore, since we have been made right in God's sight by faith, we have peace with God because of what Jesus Christ our Lord has done for us. Because of our faith, Christ has brought us into this place of undeserved privilege where we now stand, and

we confidently and joyfully look forward to sharing God's glory.

Did you see all the benefits? Did you see all the blessings? Let me highlight them while you read these verses again:

> Therefore, since we have been made right in God's sight by faith, we have **peace** with God because of what Jesus Christ our Lord has done for us. Because of our faith, Christ has brought us into this place of **undeserved privilege** where we now stand, and we **confidently and joyfully look forward to sharing God's glory**.

Do you see them now? When we are made right in God's sight through faith in His Son, we receive peace while living in God's place of undeserved privilege, and God's privilege is a life full of confidence and joy—both now and for eternity. Once we have a relationship with Christ through faith, these gifts start to take over, and for the first time our insecurities become a thing of the past.

Trust me, folks, I'm throwing you a huge gold nugget here. With these verses at the center of your life, you will be *unstoppable*. Now I didn't say you will be *untouchable*, because struggles will always be a part of life. I think a lot of people judge their Christianity by their circumstances. I can't tell you how many times I've heard people say things like "I can't be a Christian—I still struggle with addiction," or "How can I have hope for tomorrow when I don't have a job today?" or "How can I have the love of God living inside me when I don't feel love for others?" or "Why would Christ save me from my sins but not save my child from dying of cancer?"

We will always have struggles and difficult times, and it's these external challenges and wounds that drive our insecurities and ultimately cause us to lose heart and give up. But inwardly, because of our right standing with God through Christ, we are beautiful, desirable, loved, forgiven, and set free from bondage. How could Satan ever defeat a believer with that kind of confidence, a believer who lives with that kind of peace and joy in their heart? When we start to see who we are in Christ on the inside, then no satanic attack could ever bring us down.

So how do you see yourself now? Do you see what God sees as He looks at you? If not, let me try to help.

TRUE WORTH

My house is full of collectables. I have many autographs from athletes and race drivers, perhaps the most memorable being my cast that Robby Gordon, one of the best desert racers ever, signed when we raced together and I broke my arm in the 2009 Baja 1000. I have multiple footballs and baseballs signed by different athletes, as well as paintings and special books I have received from authors. I have about a hundred specialty Coke bottles, with the Coke still in them, that I collected years ago as a route salesman for Coca-Cola.

My wife calls this my junk collection, but to me these things are priceless. But as special as all these collectables are to me, nothing is more special than some roses and a Bible that I have resting all by themselves in our piano room. If you were to look at them, you might have a different opinion, wondering why I would have something like this in my home. They stand out like a sore thumb in a room full of beautiful items. They sit next to our piano, which is right next to a beautiful cabinet full of my wife's expensive Jesus figurines. Thanks to my mother, the room is stocked with nice wicker furniture and fancy paintings. And long white drapes flow all the way down to our polished wood floors. When people walk into the room, however, it's not the beautiful furnishings they notice but the roses and the Bible.

No longer red, the roses are now black. Instead of a beautiful spring smell, they carry the scent of room dust. There is no green stem full of life, but only a withered stem that is broken in several places. The accompanying baby's-breath, once full of tiny white blossoms, is nothing more than a bunch of dead, brown stems barely hanging onto the bouquet. The Bible is an old King James that is falling apart from cover to cover. Because the binding is busted, the tattered pages fall out every time you pick it up. Neither the Bible nor the bouquet appears to be worth saving.

One time when I was speaking at a youth event, I took the bouquet with me and showed it to a teenage girl and asked her if she would go out with a guy if he gave her roses like that. She took one look and said she would be offended and never talk to him again. And one time when I was speaking at a college, I showed a religion major my Bible and asked him how he would feel if someone gave it to him as a graduation gift. He took one look at it and said that after four years of hard work, including Greek and Hebrew courses, he would be very disappointed to receive a gift like that.

I can't blame them, but they don't know the true value of the roses and the Bible like I do. Why are they so special to me? Because they belonged to the greatest woman I have ever known— my grandmother.

My grandmother was a godly woman who lived a simple but powerful life. She loved the same man her whole life, and when my grandfather died she just doubled up on her service to the Lord and her family and kept on going strong. When a stroke paralyzed the right side of her body, Grandma not only taught herself to write with her left hand but began sending cards to people in the church and all over town, just to share words of God's love with them. Some of the last words she spoke, near the end of her life, expressed her concern for others who needed Jesus. She urged me to continue to pray for the lost and to love the Lord with all my heart.

At Grandma's funeral, a mentally handicapped teenager came up to me with tears in his eyes and told me that my grandmother faithfully sent him a birthday card every year, reminding him that God loved him. The roses in my piano room were on my grandmother's casket; to preserve them, I hung them upside down for a week until they dried out. The Bible that was falling apart and full of sermon notes Grandma had taken over the years was all she had to leave me.

Both of these items are priceless to me because of what they represent. I don't see roses that have lost their beauty or attractive scent; I see a life lived with integrity, service to God, and unconditional love for others. I don't see a dilapidated Bible; I see a woman who dedicated her life to prayer, studying God's Word, and selflessly sharing its truth with a lost and needy world.

LET THE WALL COME DOWN

Just as withered roses and a tattered Bible might be considered worthless based on outward appearances, you might feel similarly about yourself. If so, that's a wall of insecurity that needs to come down. You have allowed the world and Satan's outward attacks to rob you of the truth that inwardly you are a child of the Most High God. And with that truth comes all the love, grace, and forgiveness you will ever need. That truth not only results in a wall of insecurity coming down, but according to Romans 5:1–2 it also brings peace, privilege, confidence, and joy.

Do you have peace today? Do you feel like you are living a privileged life? Do you have a foundation of confidence that the world cannot shake? Do you have joy that shines like a lighthouse on a dark and stormy sea?

I must tell you, I have visited many churches in America and what I see in so many people's eyes is not peace; the worship services don't usually seem driven by lives experiencing privilege; my conversations with people don't scream out, "I'm confident in who I am in Christ"; and the attitude I sense is not the joy Paul writes about in Romans 5:3: "We can rejoice, too, when we run into problems and trials, for we know that they help us develop endurance." Notice that Paul didn't indicate that the battle on the outside would ever stop raging, but rather that we can inwardly rejoice during the storm because we know that it will develop endurance within us to help us finish the race. What's the prize at the finish line? More than you could ever imagine.

I wonder what kind of an amazing woman that teenage girl could have been if she hadn't allowed the outward attacks of some bullies to tear her down inside. I wonder how many fulfilling accomplishments my friend could have had as a husband and father, and eventually as a grandfather, if he hadn't let the stress of his circumstances drive him to the point of giving up. I wonder what kind of testimony the man who sat at the bar every day could have had if he would have allowed the love and healing of Christ to rule in his heart and help him overcome the hopelessness of his illness.

Unlike those three individuals, you still have time to make the right choice. I wonder what your life would be like if you allowed your wall of insecurity to fall down. I wonder how you would impact others' lives and change the world as you embrace Jesus in a new way.

It's important for you to have Christ in your heart and understand what that means when it comes to facing outward attacks—because, as the apostle John says, "The Spirit who lives in you is greater than the spirit who lives in the world" (1 John 4:4). Did you see that? A wall of insecurity just fell down!

Now . . . let's move on, shall we?

I Forgive You

So he returned home to his father.
And while he was still a long way off,
his father saw him coming. Filled
with love and compassion,
he ran to his son, embraced him,
and kissed him.

— Luke 15:20

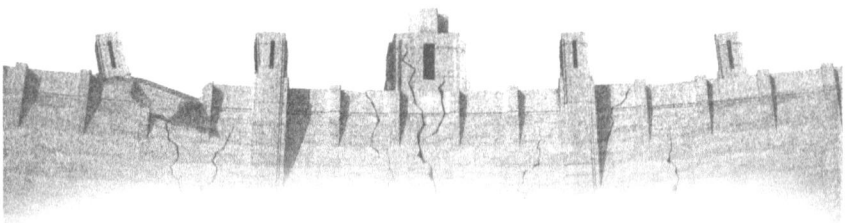

CHAPTER 4

A WALL OF UNFORGIVENESS

One day I was at home flipping through the TV channels when I came across a dramatic live courtroom scene. Sometime earlier I had heard about the case on the news. A man had been found guilty of raping and killing more than ten women. The grotesque details of the alleged crime—the suffering the guy put the victims through and the brutal way in which he ended their lives—were too much for live TV, so they decided to air only the sentencing phase of the trial. In the end he was sentenced to death row; but before the sentence was announced, the families of all the victims were given the opportunity to give the killer a piece of their mind.

I remember watching each family member approach the podium and begin hurling as many insults in the direction of the killer as they could.

"I hope you burn in hell forever!"

"I hope you get raped in prison over and over before they put you to death!"

I can't pray for you to be forgiven, but I will pray for God *not* to forgive you and to send you to eternal suffering."

"If I could get my hands on you I would make you suffer the way you made my little girl suffer!"

One after another they made their way forward to give the man their best shot. And who could blame them? But they didn't even make a dent. I watched the man on the split TV screen as he was being verbally assaulted for his crimes. He never looked at those who were speaking. He didn't even flinch, except to smile briefly during one of the attacks. You could tell his heart was as hard as stone.

But then a little elderly lady approached the podium. She had a different kind of look on her face, not displaying the intensity and aggression of those who came before her. After slowly walking up to the microphone, she paused and then said softly, "Sir, would you look at me?"

The man didn't budge. So she asked again, "Sir, would you please look at me?"

After the second request, the man slowly turned his head and looked into the woman's eyes. Then she said, "You took my little granddaughter, whom I loved with all my heart. I can't even begin to think of the things you did to her or how she spent the last few minutes of her life. But what I know I must do is forgive you for what you have done. I can't hold on to this hate, so I let it go. And I ask that God will forgive you as well."

And with that the elderly lady walked away. But not before the killer, who collapsed in an emotional breakdown, had to be carried away.

When all of the other victims' family members lashed out, the man kept his heart of stone. But when he heard words of grace and forgiveness, his heart of stone shattered.

I will never forget what I saw that day. What a clear demonstration of how powerful a weapon forgiveness is when it comes to tearing down walls. And just as forgiveness is a forceful weapon for tearing down walls, a lack of forgiveness can erect a wall that can be the demise of us and those we love.

A PROFOUND PARABLE

I'm reminded of another story in which forgiveness brought down a man's wall. We find that story in Luke's gospel, and it's too good not to share. Let's not just read it, but study it as we go.

> Jesus told them this story: "A man had two sons. The younger son told his father, 'I want my share of your estate now before you die.' So his father agreed to divide his wealth between his sons." – Luke 15:11–12

It's important to note here that the young man's request was the same as saying he wished his father was dead so that he could have his money, but since his father wasn't dead he wanted to get his inheritance early. Can you imagine the pain that went along with that request? The father doesn't seem to take it personally, though, since he divides up his estate so that his younger son could have his share. (Following the custom of the day, the older brother would receive a double portion, getting two-thirds of the estate while the younger brother would get one-third.)

"A few days later this younger son packed all his be-
longings and moved to a distant land, and there he
wasted all his money on wild living. About the time
his money ran out, a great famine swept over the land,
and he began to starve." – Luke 15:13–14

Here Jesus' parable illustrates how the world will turn its back
on you. The young man had no sooner slid from the rich and
famous to the broke and miserable when a famine swept over the
land and the struggle intensified times ten. If you have made a bad
choice, the world is not where your rescue will come from. The
world won't pick you up when have fallen or set you free if you
are in bondage, but rather will stomp out the little bit of life you
have left.

I meet so many people who turn their hearts toward the world
without realizing that when the good times run out and they have
nothing to offer the world back, the good times will dramatically come to an end. Another way to say it is that the world is
very unforgiving.

"He persuaded a local farmer to hire him, and the
man sent him into his fields to feed the pigs. The
young man became so hungry that even the pods he
was feeding the pigs looked good to him. But no one
gave him anything." – Luke 15:15–16

No one was helping the young man. No one was giving him
anything. Instead, they watched him suffer and starve because of
his past choices. Again, the world is very unforgiving.

The point I want to make here in relation to tearing down
walls is that it is extremely difficult to see a wall fall if you stay
connected to the world. That's why the apostle Peter referred to

believers as "temporary residents and foreigners" (1 Peter 2:11)—
people who are focused on the eternal rather than the temporary.

> "When he finally came to his senses, he said to himself,
> 'At home even the hired servants have food enough to
> spare, and here I am dying of hunger! I will go home
> to my father and say, "Father, I have sinned against
> both heaven and you, and I am no longer worthy of
> being called your son. Please take me on as a hired
> servant."'" – Luke 15:17–19

The young man is in the right frame of mind now, ready to
move forward and start anew. But notice the wound the world has
caused. The prodigal rehearses these words to speak to his father: "I
am no longer worthy of being called your son." Because of his bad
choices, he thinks he has to be a slave for the rest of his days. And
living without freedom eventually drains the soul.

This is what a wall looks like in our lives. I constantly see people walking around with this look of slavery on their face, plodding
through life with a gaping wound that the world will continue to
infect. My greatest desire in writing this book is to see those walls
of slavery fall down so that God's people can walk in freedom.

Let's come back to Jesus' parable, because the prodigal son
is about to see a wall fall down and experience freedom from his
past mistakes.

> "So he returned home to his father. And while he
> was still a long way off, his father saw him coming.
> Filled with love and compassion, he ran to his son,
> embraced him, and kissed him. His son said to him,
> 'Father, I have sinned against both heaven and you,
> and I am no longer worthy of being called your son.'

"But his father said to the servants, 'Quick! Bring the finest robe in the house and put it on him. Get a ring for his finger and sandals for his feet. And kill the calf we have been fattening. We must celebrate with a feast, for this son of mine was dead and has now returned to life. He was lost, but now he is found.' So the party began." – Luke 15:20–24

I love this exchange. But my favorite part is that the father didn't allow his son to finish the apology speech he had prepared. To complete the speech, the son had planned to say, "Please take me on as a hired servant." But that statement would have thrown him back into slavery, and the father would have none of it.

PARTY PERKS

Jesus is making a beautiful point here. God's intent is not for us to be in bondage but rather to be set free from our past mistakes—our sins—and have a hope that goes beyond our failures. How are we going to get there? The same way the son did: through the forgiveness of the Father. And we need to understand that there is a huge payoff once we get there. It's worth confronting and conquering our walls. It's worth the blood, sweat, and tears that will be shed along the way. It's worth fighting the battle that sets us free.

Let's check out the payoff Jesus illustrated with His story. I love Jesus' closing words: "So the party began." This party was loaded with great perks, to say the least. The special robe that was put on the young man was always worn by the guest of honor. So the prodigal son who was recently hanging out with pigs was now the number-one guest. The ring would be worn by the person in charge or by one who was seen as a high authority. The young man went from taking orders to giving them. And sandals were never worn by slaves, who always went barefoot. This signified that the son's days of slavery were over and he had stepped into full freedom.

The difference Jesus was making between the two lives is staggering. This young man who had just been desiring to eat what he was feeding pigs—an unspeakable indignity for any self-respecting Jew—went from that miserable existence to a life full of acceptance, honor, and authority. It makes you wonder why anyone wouldn't want to receive forgiveness so a wall could fall down. And in addition to that, why would anyone withhold forgiveness from others who have been kept in bondage over past mistakes and prevent them from receiving this kind of welcome home?

You might be asking yourself if I really know what I'm talking about on this one. Let me assure you that I do. So you know I have walked this path and learned from it, I'm going to share a bit of my own prodigal days.

MYRTLE BEACH PRODIGAL

Myrtle Beach, South Carolina is a wonderful vacation spot. People go there to relax in the sun and be replenished of the life that has been drained out of them by their daily routine. But for me Myrtle Beach is nothing more than a reminder of how bad life can get.

In the days just before I became a Christ-follower, when I was seventeen years old, this place filled with beautiful sand beaches and golf courses was where I walked the streets homeless and begged for food because I had squandered everything I possessed. This safe haven of family fun and entertainment was where a man pulled a gun on me in the middle of the night and made me beg for my life. This place loaded with five-star resorts was where I had a severe drug reaction that landed me in the hospital, clinging to life.

Myrtle Beach will always represent the place where I needed a father's love the most—and found it. It was there that I decided to humble myself, craft my apology speech, and head back home. Hard times had so squashed my pride that I was ready to ask my dad if I could return home. Wondering if he would choose to forgive me, the scenarios I imagined in my mind didn't always play out in my favor. I was willing to lay it all on the line, though, because I was dying physically and didn't know how much longer I could hang on before doing something that would cost me everything.

All my questions were answered, however, the night I was walking down the street and my dad came looking for me. I ran up to him and started to apologize. But I was quickly interrupted by these four words: "Son, I forgive you." Those words changed my life in such a powerful way that every time I go to Myrtle Beach to vacation or speak I get teary-eyed thinking about my father not letting his son go without experiencing the party.

Because of God's forgiveness, an eternal home awaits me where I will be wearing a robe of honor, a ring of authority, and sandals of freedom. Is this the party that awaits you one day? Are you adorned with these precious party gifts now?

My earthly father's forgiveness has had a dramatic impact on my life. Just like the father in the parable of the prodigal son, my dad neither made me work for forgiveness nor struck me with words that I'm sure I deserved. Instead, he forgave me immediately and with no strings attached. That was a game-changer for me then and it still is today. As a result, I have been able to offer forgiveness to those who have wounded me; I remember the day I needed it, and I remember the feeling that accompanied being forgiven and set free.

A FATHER'S LOVE

Something else I will never forget is holding my firstborn son, Malachi, in my arms for the first time. Standing in that hospital in Greenville, South Carolina, I heard God speak to me so clearly that I thought everyone else heard it too. "Christian, if your son turned out to be a thief, would you still love and forgive him? If he turned out to be a murderer, would you still love and forgive him? If he turned out to be a drunkard, or a womanizer, would you still love and forgive him? If he turned out to be gay, would you still love and forgive him? If he turned out to be the worst of all things, would you still love him and forgive him?"

With tears in my eyes, I answered out loud, "Yes, Lord, You know I will."

I then felt that God was showing me I had been set free with this kind of love and forgiveness and that I was called to offer it not only to my son but to others in the world who seek love in all the wrong places.

I wonder if we have forgotten how to preach and to practice love and forgiveness in the church today. Maybe that's why the bars are packed on Friday and Saturday night and people are too hung over and tired to go hear about Jesus on Sunday morning. Or maybe when they decided to visit a church they experienced something like I did about a year ago.

A CHURCH BRAWL

Scheduled to preach a weeklong "revival," I walked into the church building for the initial service on Sunday morning. Instantly I could sense that everyone was angry. I tried to find someone who could tell me what was going on, but everyone seemed completely consumed by frustration. Finally, one of the elders pulled me aside and told me they had fired the pastor the night before and people were just now finding out. The young pastor was outgoing and evangelistic, which made a lot of the older folks nervous. They didn't like his style, his zeal, and his passionate preaching that went ten minutes past noon, putting them at the back of the line at the K&W Cafeteria. So they decided to get rid of him.

Since I had been brought in to preach a revival at the young pastor's invitation, I was quite uncomfortable with the situation. But I decided to honor my commitment to the church and go ahead and preach. I prayed and felt that God put a message of forgiveness on my heart, which I thought I preached to perfection. It obviously didn't work, though, because as soon as I was done the people gathered at the back—the younger ones on one side and the older ones on the other—and started to let each other have it.

I left very frustrated, praying that no visitors had shown up that day, and headed to the Hickory Tavern to watch the Talladega Race on FOX Sports and eat some wings. Right about the time my food came, my wife called and asked how it went that morning. And then before I had time to answer her question, Amy asked about all the noise in the background. I informed her that it was a rough morning, and the noise she was hearing was because I was hanging out at a bar. Everyone there was getting along fine—while the church members were about to kill each other!

All week I preached and gave altar calls pertaining to forgiveness. But no one chose to tear down a wall. They walked away with malice in their hearts toward other brothers and sisters, and the wall never fell. They rejected forgiveness—and therefore never received it either.

RECEIVING AND GIVING FORGIVENESS

You might be wondering how I could make such a bold statement about God not forgiving those who have not forgiven others. Do I know what is in a person's heart? No. But I do know what Jesus said on this subject.

"Pray like this:

Our Father in heaven,
 may your name be kept holy.
May your Kingdom come soon.
May your will be done on earth,
 as it is in heaven.
Give us today the food we need,
and forgive us our sins,
 as we have forgiven those who sin against us.
And don't let us yield to temptation,
 but rescue us from the evil one.

"If you forgive those who sin against you, your heavenly Father will forgive you. But if you refuse to forgive others, your Father will not forgive your sins."
– Matthew 6:9–15

Many elements have to come together for a wall to be built. In addition to the bricks, you need concrete mix, sand, and water in order to make mortar. And just as there is more than one step to building a wall, there is more than one step—when it comes to forgiveness—to tearing it down. We have been called not only to receive forgiveness by repenting of our sins but also to give forgiveness to others, which links us to grace itself.

Where are you at with this forgiveness thing? Are you still holding on to something from the past? Have you refused to forgive yourself for something you did years ago? Did someone do something to you that you have never forgiven them for? Do you make others work hard to get your forgiveness, keeping them in slavery for the mistakes they have made?

One thing is for sure, you can bet that Jesus was serious when He talked about forgiveness and eternity. Forgiveness can bring down a wall and set you free from yourself, which I promise is the best news you will ever hear. But withholding forgiveness will keep you enslaved. There is no forgiveness for Satan, so you know he tries to keep this message far from us as well.

Is the wall crumbling yet? What are you waiting for?

THE SILENT KILLER

Looking at the man, Jesus felt genuine love for him. "There is still one thing you haven't done," he told him. "Go and sell all your possessions and give the money to the poor, and you will have treasure in heaven. Then come, follow me."

– Mark 10:21

CHAPTER 5

A WALL OF COMPLACENCY

Recently our nation has seen a lot of silent but deadly killers. Aimee Copeland, a twenty-four-year-old graduate student at the University of West Georgia, fell from a broken zip-line into the Little Tallapoosa River and suffered a deep cut in her leg. She contracted necrotizing fasciitis, a flesh-eating bacterial disease, and three days later her leg had to be amputated. Fortunately Aimee's life was spared and she is making a full recovery, but not before her other foot and both of her hands had to be amputated as well.

Excited moviegoers in Aurora, Colorado (which is where Kingdom Building Ministries, the ministry I'm affiliated with, is located) filled a theater to see the midnight opening of the final *Batman* film, *The Dark Knight Rises*. Waiting silently outside the theater was James Holmes, a young man with an arsenal of weapons who was plotting to ambush innocent men, women, and children.

A few months later another young man, Adam Lanza, walked into Sandy Hook Elementary School in Newtown, Connecticut and opened fire on students and teachers. Before killing himself, Lanza had killed twenty children and six adults.

And as I write this chapter we are but a few days removed from yet another act of terrorism in America. Two young men carried backpacks containing homemade bombs into the crowd lined up to watch the Boston Marathon. The spectators had no idea that near their feet a silent killer was waiting to strike—taking the lives of three people and injuring scores of others.

Another tragic silent killer is plaguing our churches in America today. That silent killer is complacency.

THE RICH YOUNG RULER

A well-known story from Jesus' life provides an example of this silent killer.

> As Jesus was starting out on his way to Jerusalem, a man came running up to him, knelt down, and asked, "Good Teacher, what must I do to inherit eternal life?"
>
> "Why do you call me good?" Jesus asked. "Only God is truly good. But to answer your question, you know the commandments: 'You must not murder. You must not commit adultery. You must not steal. You must not testify falsely. You must not cheat anyone. Honor your father and mother.'"
>
> "Teacher," the man replied, "I've obeyed all these commandments since I was young."
>
> Looking at the man, Jesus felt genuine love for him. "There is still one thing you haven't done," he

told him. "Go and sell all your possessions and give the money to the poor, and you will have treasure in heaven. Then come, follow me."

At this the man's face fell, and he went away sad, for he had many possessions. – Mark 10:17–22

Based on combining the accounts in Matthew, Mark, and Luke, this man has come to be known as the "rich young ruler." He was obviously rich; Matthew 19:20 tells us he was young; and Luke 18:18 (in some translations) refers to him as a "ruler," which likely means that he was a member of an official Jewish council or court.

This good man, whom Jesus loved, had the potential to change the world. But he was afflicted by a silent killer that he didn't even know existed. What makes complacency so deadly is that, like a lethal virus, it can sometimes stay hidden for years until it bursts into activity, attacking its host as well as many others.

Why do I think this man struggled with complacency more than greed? After Jesus directed the man to give away his wealth, He told him to "come, follow me." There is nothing easy about following Jesus, nothing safe about making Christ our Lord, nothing pleasant about taking up our cross and suffering for Him. As I like to say, it's a radical, dramatical, fanatical walk of faith into the unknown. I don't believe this man's struggle was with greed so much as it was with the drastic step of faith it would take to give everything up and walk with Jesus in a life of sacrifice. A wall of complacency needed to come down in his life.

Is confronting this wall and seeing it come down worth the pain that will be required? Think about this. Because Jesus invited this man to come and follow Him, we can assume that he could have . . .

- witnessed the wonderful healings that Jesus performed
- tasted the fish and bread that Jesus miraculously fed the multitudes
- watched with awe as demons were cast out by the legion
- known the thrill of encountering the risen Christ
- experienced the transforming power of the Holy Spirit on the day of Pentecost
- shared in the glory of Jesus' suffering and death

But rather than taking advantage of all these great opportunities, this man's story has an unhappy ending. After he heard Jesus' challenging words, "The man's face fell, and he went away sad, for he had many possessions" (Mark 10:22). What potential this rich man possessed. He could have been great in God's kingdom. But instead he walked away sad—never to be mentioned again in Scripture.

Why do so many churchgoers today walk away, in essence, from Jesus?

Look again at the last thing the rich man missed out on: sharing in the glory of Jesus' suffering and death. Perhaps you winced a bit when you read that the first time. Many churches in America are filled with people on Sunday mornings, but I wonder how full they would be if Jesus showed up and told them to give everything away and follow Him. I wonder how many would sign up if He told them, as He did Peter in John 21, that following Him would cost them their lives. I wonder how many would volunteer to be the next martyr after watching Stephen get stoned to death for speaking out about Jesus. I wonder how many would profess their faith openly if they knew what awaited them was being torn to pieces by lions in the "games" at the coliseum in Rome or burned alive as torches to illuminate Nero's gardens.

I think we all know how these scenarios would play out. But here's what we don't understand. Jesus calls for a radical response—"If you do not carry your own cross and follow me, you cannot be my disciple" (Luke 14:27). We don't realize that dodging suffering doesn't bring us the happiness we are looking for; it actually robs us of the fullness of life that Christ intends for us.

AVOIDING THE ALLIGATORS

I'm reminded of a story a young man shared with me during a conference in which I was speaking. A friend of his had recently gone to Zimbabwe to go whitewater rafting. In the United States, any water past Class 5 is deemed too dangerous to brave and is therefore illegal. But in Zimbabwe they let you ride Class 6 rapids if you have the guts. While the professional guide was briefing his friend about all the rules he needed to follow to keep safe, the guide said, "When you get thrown from the raft you must stay where the current is raging the most."

His friend asked the guide why he said "*When* you get thrown from the raft" instead of "*If* you get thrown from the raft."

"You *will* get thrown from the raft," the guide responded. "And when you do, you must stay where the current is raging the most rather than swimming to the shore where the water is calm."

Persisting, the young American asked why he shouldn't swim to calm water. The guide responded, "Because where the water is calm, is where the alligators will be waiting to eat you."

Apparently the alligators can't attack where the current is strong, but they can get you where the water is calm. That is a great illustration of the realities of the Christian life. Rather than being calm and safe, following Jesus is radical and dangerous.

I will admit that I'm like all those today who would rather skip the whole suffering process and live a life of comfort and leisure. But to imagine sadly walking away from Jesus, as did the rich young ruler, reminds me that I want to look back when my time comes and realize that I laid it all on the line for Christ—making a difference in the world and leaving a legacy.

It amazes me that the Bible's teachings in regard to suffering and radical living seem to have escaped the pulpit today, being replaced by a complacent, don't-rock-the-boat theology and lifestyle. Have we forgotten the heroes of our faith?

- Abraham was willing to raise his knife to slay his son as proof of his faith (see Genesis 22:10).
- A lad by the name of David let an army full of cowards know that he, for one, wasn't afraid of a nine-foot tall giant: "Who is this pagan Philistine anyway, that he is allowed to defy the armies of the living God" (1 Samuel 17:26).
- Shadrach, Meshach, and Abednego stood their ground against their pagan captor and the world's most powerful king: "O Nebuchadnezzar, we do not need to defend ourselves before you. If we are thrown into the blazing furnace, the God whom we serve is able to save us. He will rescue us from your power, Your Majesty. But even if he doesn't, we want to make it clear to you, Your Majesty, that we will never serve your gods or worship the gold statue you have set up" (Daniel 3:16–18).
- In an effort to save her people, Esther approached the king, knowing that doing so could mean death (see Esther 4:11). "If I must die, I must die," she proclaimed (Esther 4:16).
- Peter got out of the boat and walked on the choppy water of the Sea of Galilee (see Matthew 14:29).

- Paul was warned by the Holy Spirit "in city after city that jail and suffering lie ahead." Yet he declared, "But my life is worth nothing to me unless I use it for finishing the work assigned me by the Lord Jesus—the work of telling others the Good News about the wonderful grace of God" (Acts 20:23–24).

Though our churches today are rife with complacency, we have these stories of how people of faith have always lived out a radical calling. And why is it that radical living always attracts the most attention? Because a message sealed in the blood, sweat, and tears of the messenger is the most trustworthy and respected. What seals the deal for me is that the disciples lost their lives for what they believed and professed, which certainly wouldn't have happened had it all been a lie. I contend that we need to get rid of the wall of complacency in our churches and personal lives and see what God can do with a little crazy Christianity.

BAJA BOUND

When I was a child, my father was a successful professional motorcycle racer. One of my earliest memories is sitting in the stands at Daytona when I was four years old while my mom pointed out my dad to me as he went around the racetrack. My dad was always my hero, and I wanted to be just like him.

I started riding motorcycles at a very young age. My mom has a picture of me riding a Z50 Honda when I was just three-and-a-half years old—without a shirt and my blonde hair flapping in the breeze underneath my helmet. As I grew older I continued to ride, embracing the joy that comes with going fast. Several years ago I even had the opportunity to be on the Spike TV reality show,

Reality Racing: The Rookie Challenge, and ended up winning the show and picking up the nickname "The Faster Pastor."

In 2009 I decided to enter the most dangerous race in the world, the Baja 1000. Held every November on Mexico's Baja California Peninsula, the course traverses some of the most perilous off-road terrain on the planet. Unfortunately, it's not unusual for contestants (and/or spectators) to be killed in high-speed crashes.

My desire to participate in the race was sparked by the movie *Dust to Glory.* But along with the high speeds and danger that accompany the race, I was also drawn to the opportunity to visit orphanages in different parts of Baja that have had little exposure to the gospel. I started to raise money and recruit some men to go with me, both for the race and to do ministry along the way. I knew it was a God thing when we built a team of talented guys and raised ten thousand dollars in just a short amount of time.

One person, however, wasn't so excited about my venture. A really good pastor friend of mine kept telling me that I was going to die. From time to time he would call to say he had a vision from God that I wasn't going to make it back home, so I better change my plans and stay home for the sake of my wife and three kids. I responded that I felt that the ministry we were going to do would make the trip worth the risks. As the time came for us to travel to Baja, he continued to warn me that death and destruction awaited me.

MAKING A DIFFERENCE

When we got to Mexico, we realized that the rumors we had heard about the drug cartels causing havoc across the border were true. We saw the evidence of prostitution, thievery, deception, and murder. Yet we experienced a great opportunity to share the gospel and make a difference for the kingdom. In the five short days we were there, we gave out a thousand Bibles and witnessed to many people who had never heard the message of Jesus—giving us a chance to tell those who felt unloved and lost that God loves them unconditionally and that there is hope for a better life.

When the ministry phase ended and the race began, I immediately realized that although I still had the competitive fire to go fast, I had lost much of the coordination I possessed in my younger days. Less than ten miles into the race I crashed, breaking my hand and my arm. There I lay in the Mexican desert with a crushed throttle hand and a crooked arm. But determined to finish what I started, I got back on the bike and finished my section of the race. After I handed off the bike to the next rider on our team, the race emergency staff began the process of transporting me out of the desert. I declined their offer to take me to a hospital, requesting instead that they take me to my hotel in Ensenada, where the Baja began.

When I called my wife to tell her what happened, she encouraged me to do my best to man up and drive four days back across the country before going to the hospital, so that our insurance would cover my injuries. Since the rest of our team flew to and from the race, I drove by myself the whole way home, with my arm elevated, and then went to an orthopedic doctor in Charlotte.

After I got home, my buddy called to see how things went. When I told him about my wreck, he rubbed it in that he had told me this was going to happen and that I should have stayed home like he said. I retorted that he didn't tell me I was going to break my hand and arm but that I was going to be killed—which made him a false prophet!

We both had a good laugh, but then our conversation turned more serious as he stated that at my age I really did need to stick to safer ways to share the message of Jesus. At that point I shared with him about our ministry opportunities. How we had given out a thousand Bibles to people who were in need of reading the message of hope through God's truth. How at orphanages in the remote Baja desert I had held children in my arms who had never felt the love and touch of a Christian man. How our team had witnessed to those walking the streets in Ensenada and San Felipe, as well as to the spectators who had gathered along the race course to watch the riders go by.

I told him about the waitress we met who had just lost her mother and now her father was forcing her to work, even though she was just a young teenager, to help support the family. I shared how we loved on her and I gave her a racing jersey.

I was able to report how we gained the respect of racers from the West Coast who cross the border every year to spend time partying and breaking all the rules. (If what happens in Vegas stays in Vegas, then what happens in Mexico *definitely* stays in Mexico.) In fact, one West Coast racer who had been competing in the Baja 1000 for over ten years, and had even won it one year, mentioned that hanging out with us had kept him out of the strip clubs and away from the drugs and alcohol for the first time.

Finally, I told my friend how I sped faster than one hundred miles per hour in the desert of Mexico and then came riding out of the desert just in time to watch the sun set on the shore at San Felipe. And then I asked, "What did you do last week?"

There was silence on the other end of the phone for a moment. And then he said, "Not that."

The truth is that he probably followed his normal routine: working in his office, studying for his sermon, doing some research on the Internet, answering a few phone calls, having a couple of lunch meetings with people on his staff, playing a round of golf, and hanging out with his family. Is there anything wrong with that? Not necessarily. It's not wrong to stay in the boat, and it's not wrong to jump out of the boat. But we all have to discern what consumes our lives. Are we driven by complacency or by the desire to be bold and radical in our faith?

If you're like me, you sure don't want to look back someday and realize you could have, should have, or would have done more . . . but you didn't.

WILL YOU FIGHT?

As I conclude this chapter, I realize—much to my shame—that I haven't used a quote from the movie *Braveheart* yet in this book. So let's finish with one that challenges complacency.

Before the first big battle between the Scots and the English, William Wallace (played by Mel Gibson) faces his fellow soldiers who are ready to retreat and live in slavery to the English. Contending with a wall of complacency, they are willing to settle for a life of second-best and what-ifs. Wallace responds to this challenge with the most memorable and inspiring speech of the movie.

"I am William Wallace! And I see a whole army of my countrymen here in defiance of tyranny. You have come to fight as free men, and free men you are. What will you do with that freedom? Will you fight?"

"Fight? Against that?" one of the scared Scottish soldiers replies. "No, we will run. And we will live."

Then Wallace says, "Aye, fight and you may die. Run, and you will live . . . at least a while. And dying in your beds, many years from now, would you be willing to trade all the days, from this day to that, for one chance, just one chance, to come back here and tell our enemies that they may take our lives but they will never take *our freedom*?!"

Remember, the whole purpose of tearing down walls is to escape bondage and be free in Christ. And we need to understand that freedom cannot be obtained with a life of complacency.

The rich young ruler walked away thinking it was better to keep his wall up. But Scripture tells us that he walked away sad. I wonder if he wished, on his deathbed, that he could go back to the day he met Jesus and trade all his remaining days for the life he would have had if he had chosen to give it all up and follow the Master?

Say yes to Jesus and no to complacency—today!

SHADOWS

God has said, "I will never fail you.
I will never abandon you."
So we can say with confidence,
"The Lord is my helper, so I will
have no fear. What can mere
people do to me?"

– Hebrews 13:5–6

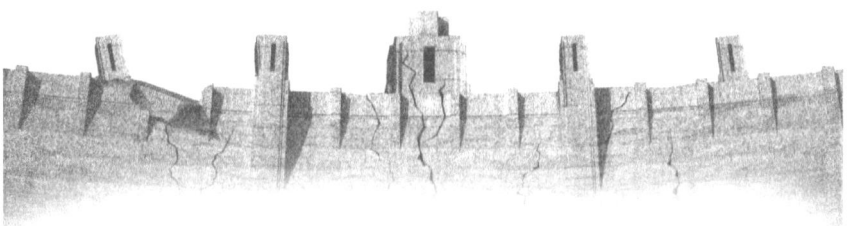

CHAPTER 6

A WALL OF FEAR

When I was growing up, I had the typical childhood fears of shadows and darkness. That fear kept me from sleeping many nights, as I stared into the dark closet waiting for something to attack. That fear kept me from listening to campfire stories as a Boy Scout. That fear kept me from exploring the dark caves behind my house with my friends. That fear kept me from playing in the attic of my grandparents' farmhouse with my cousins. And though I can laugh about it now, that fear kept me from going on the Haunted Mansion ride at Disney World!

Like most kids, I outgrew my fear of shadowy darkness. Unfortunately, however, I developed more serious fears later in life.

During my teen years I got involved in dealing drugs, sorry to say. One night I was driving home alone during a drug run to Charlotte when I decided to sample some of the product, which soon proved to be a bad idea. Within an hour, somewhere around

Conway, South Carolina, my heart started palpitating and I became short of breath.

I tried to find a hospital by looking for signs on the highway, but my vision was becoming blurry. As my body continued to react violently to the drugs in my system, I began to try to make peace with death. But then I saw a blue sign with an H on it and was able to find my way to the emergency room. It was about 2 a.m. when I practically crawled through the front door.

As medical personnel hurried to take care of me, my memory of the night becomes blank. When I woke up the next day, a nurse told me I was lucky to be alive. She said I could leave whenever I was ready, but before I was discharged she recommended some rehab centers and counselors that could give me the help I needed.

The Dread of Driving

I left the hospital thinking that the worst of my fears were over, but the worst was yet to come—and it wasn't from drugs. Because I was in the car alone when I had my near-death experience, I became afraid to be alone while driving a car. Nearly every time I drove a considerable distance by myself, I had a panic attack.

If you have never experienced a full-blown panic attack, you should feel blessed, because they are terribly frightening and absolutely controlling. Mine would always be the same: My throat would tighten up until I couldn't swallow, my heart would palpitate wildly, and my breathing would become so labored that I would eventually be gasping for air. After a while I decided I wouldn't be in the car alone. If I couldn't find someone to go with me, I wouldn't go.

I got along OK until I became a traveling speaker and repeatedly needed to travel alone. I wish I could tell you I was brave and overcame my fear, but the truth is that if my wife couldn't go with me, I would usually turn down an invitation. This wall of fear had so consumed my mind and heart that I was turning down opportunities to preach the gospel because I was scared to be alone in the car.

That is what a wall of fear will always do—not only keep you from success but impact others' success as well. It is very painful yet today for me to think about all the opportunities to share the life-giving message of experiencing God's love through a relationship with Christ that I forfeited because I was enslaved by my wall of fear. How many people could have connected with my testimony and the preaching of the gospel that I so passionately love? I allowed my wall of fear to affect the lives of others, which I still regret.

Well, eventually the time came for me to confront my wall of fear. I have several accountability partners. One is Adrian Despres, who played football at Furman University and is 6'5" and 245 pounds. Another is Foster Christy, who was a star fullback at Auburn University and is 6'4" and 255 pounds. But my 5'6", 135-pound wife can keep me in line better than anyone. One day I told Amy that I had received an invitation to speak but she was working, and I didn't want to go because I was scared I would have a panic attack and hyperventilate if I went in the car alone.

If you're thinking I'm going to say that my gentle, loving Proverbs-31 wife smiled and said, "Baby, just get there if you can," you're wrong. Amy told me to cowboy up and stop allowing Satan to have the victory in my life. She said that people would be there who needed to hear what I had to say about Jesus, and I shouldn't let them down. After hearing more encouraging words from my wife for me to be the man God created me to be, I decided to confront my fear. So off I went, with tears in my eyes, trying to hold it together.

While I was driving down the road I tried listening to music and going over my sermon notes in my head. But since nothing would take my mind off the fear, not long into my journey I started having a panic attack. I was short of breath, my throat was tightening, and my chest was hurting. So I pulled off the road and began to cry and pray. I was about to turn around and head for home when I sensed God saying to me, "Look in the passenger seat. Is anyone there?"

"No, Lord," I cried out, "no one is there."

OPENED EYES

To help convey what happened next, let's look at a passage from 2 Kings:

> When the king of Aram was at war with Israel, he would confer with his officers and say, "We will mobilize our forces at such and such a place."
>
> But immediately Elisha, the man of God, would warn the king of Israel, "Do not go near that place, for the Arameans are planning to mobilize their troops there." So the king of Israel would send word to the place indicated by the man of God. Time and again Elisha warned the king, so that he would be on the alert there.
>
> The king of Aram became very upset over this. He called his officers together and demanded, "Which of you is the traitor? Who has been informing the king of Israel of my plans?"
>
> "It's not us, my lord the king," one of the officers replied. "Elisha, the prophet in Israel, tells the king

of Israel even the words you speak in the privacy of your bedroom!"

"Go and find out where he is," the king commanded, "so I can send troops to seize him."

And the report came back: "Elisha is at Dothan." So one night the king of Aram sent a great army with many chariots and horses to surround the city.

When the servant of the man of God got up early the next morning and went outside, there were troops, horses, and chariots everywhere. "Oh, sir, what will we do now?" the young man cried to Elisha.

"Don't be afraid!" Elisha told him. "For there are more on our side than on theirs!" Then Elisha prayed, "O LORD, open his eyes and let him see!" The LORD opened the young man's eyes, and when he looked up, he saw that the hillside around Elisha was filled with horses and chariots of fire. – 2 Kings 6:8–17

Elisha's servant, like me, was staring at a wall of fear. And he experienced a victory very similar to the one I was about to experience. When I cried out that no one was in the passenger seat of my car, God opened my eyes and allowed me to sense His presence. I realized that I would never be alone because He would always be with me wherever I was called to go.

Ever since then, His presence has broken down that wall of fear. I have never had another hyperventilating panic attack while driving a car alone or while flying on a plane alone. I give the Lord all the praise for this wall coming down. And I want you to know that your wall of fear can come crashing down too.

I do need to admit, however, that I continue to deal with fear. It seems like I obtain victory in one area only to see Satan gather his demonic angels for yet another charge. According to 1 John

4:16–18, "God is love" and His "perfect love expels all fear." Satan knows he can never take God's love away from us, but he continues to try to build a wall of fear in our lives in order to keep us from *feeling* that love. Then he can significantly hinder our testimonies and our ability to advance God's kingdom.

A YEAR OF FEAR

Let me illustrate this by recounting the year of fear I endured in 2009. It started when I was in El Salvador with a team from Kingdom Building Ministries and several missionaries from Compassion International. Things were going great as we connected with the lost, loved on those who needed to be encouraged with Christ's love, and gave away basic provisions to sustain those in need.

I was having a great time playing soccer with some kids when my competitive edge got me in trouble. While I was racing a teenager up a hill, I suddenly felt something explode in my right ankle. Because I have suffered many broken bones while racing motorcycles, when I saw that my foot was dangling and I couldn't move my toes, my first thought was that my ankle had sustained a compound fracture. I lifted up my pant leg, expecting to see some blood and protruding bones; but that wasn't the case. Then I pressed on the back of my heel and realized I had completely severed my Achilles tendon, which was coiled up in a knot in my calf.

I took the next flight from El Salvador to Charlotte, where the doctor who does surgeries for the Carolina Panthers repaired my Achilles tendon. I spent the next month lying on the couch with my leg elevated, eating Cocoa Pebbles and watching ESPN. I gained about twenty pounds, and we ended up buying a new couch because I ruined the springs in the old one from lying on it so much.

The time finally came for me to get my walking boot, and the doctor said I was good to go with my rehab. That night I walked upstairs to sleep in my own bed for the first time in over a month. I turned off the light, took off my walking boot, and started making my way to the bed. Unbelievably, at that moment I stepped on a *Star Wars* R2-D2 toy. An all-too familiar pain shot through my lower leg, and I was sure that I had snapped my Achilles tendon again.

I would love to say that a praise song rang out of my mouth, but I will simply mention that in Matthew 26:74 Peter swore. After my reaction woke up everyone in the house, I grabbed R2-D2, slung him across the room, and screamed, "The force is *not* with me!!" Amy still teases me for saying that; but that night everyone steered clear of me while I curled up in the fetal position on our bedroom floor and cried for an hour.

The next day I went to the doctor, and my greatest fears were confirmed. I had partially torn my Achilles tendon again; and because of my age and all the scar tissue caused by the initial injury, surgery wasn't an option. My Achilles would never be the same. That was very difficult for me to hear, especially since I had been an athlete my whole life and much of my confidence had come from what I had accomplished on the field of competition. The familiar effects of fear flooded over me as I contemplated what this would mean for my self-esteem and my future. I felt handicapped.

That feeling was confirmed by the doctor, who told me that years ago prison guards would cut their prisoners' Achilles tendons so that they couldn't run away to escape. Then the doctor asked me if I was running away from something and if God might be trying to teach me a lesson. To be honest, at the time I didn't know if he was right or not, and I didn't even care. It was rather aggravating to pay close to twenty grand to listen to someone give me an object lesson.

MORE TRIALS

The fateful year of 2009 rolled along, but my trials were far from over. One day while I was speaking at a youth conference in Gatlinburg, Tennessee, my father called to tell me he had gone to the doctor and that he just found out he had terminal cancer. What?! I remember sitting on the edge of the bed in my hotel room wondering how I was going to stand in front of a bunch of teenagers and tell them about God's love when I didn't feel that love myself.

Here I was again—about to let fear keep me from sharing God's Word.

Fortunately, I was able to pray through and keep going, fighting to trust God and not allow Satan to rebuild a wall of fear in my life. But then my wife and I went on a date and she handed me a piece of paper she had received in the mail informing her that her last breast exam revealed she possibly had cancer.

I started to cry, telling Amy that if anything happened to her I didn't know how I could raise our boys and continue serving the Lord in ministry. Amy, being the strong woman of God that she is, told me I should pray, trust, and never give up on what God had called me to do. Her words reminded me of what she had told me years earlier, standing in our kitchen in Central, South Carolina, when I was too scared to travel without her being with me.

Not long after that I received a call from a man who identified himself as a state trooper and then asked if I was Kay Chapman's son. When I said yes, he told me that my mother had an aneurysm, which caused her to fall off her sundeck, break her neck, and become paralyzed.

I couldn't believe what I was hearing—I mean, what's next?! I hurried home to find my mom lying in the emergency room with tears in her eyes, saying that she couldn't feel anything below her neck and fearing that she would never walk again.

The following week I was scheduled to travel to Mexico, both to race in the Baja 1000 as well as to share the message of Christ and hand out Bibles. Because my mom was lying in the hospital, paralyzed by her injuries, I considered canceling the trip. But after crying a little and praying a lot, I decided I shouldn't let this keep me from completing what God had opened the door for me to do. I could feel my throat tightening up and my heart beating faster as I was reminded yet again of my previous fears that had propelled me to run away rather than to finish the race for Christ.

Well, you know from the previous chapter how my Baja race turned out. While I was lying in Mexico with a broken hand and a broken arm, reviewing everything that had happened to me in 2009, I have to admit that I wanted to give up. I was ready to unpack my sleeping bag, curl up behind my wall of fear, and check out. I felt too rejected to experience God's love, too isolated to receive His grace, and too unworthy to be called His child.

Had I been rejected by God? Was I isolated from His grace? Was I unworthy of being called His child? Absolutely not. But again, that is the kind of attack Satan unleashes on our lives—attempting, through fear, to make us feel separated from God's perfect love.

Feeling myself beginning to hyperventilate and to allow past walls of fear to be rebuilt in my life, I started to sing God's praise:

> Amazing grace! How sweet the sound
> That saved a wretch like me!

I once was lost, but now am found;
Was blind, but now I see.

In that moment of singing God's praise I began to focus on Christ's unconditional love for me and the fact that He has a plan for my life despite the attack of the enemy. No matter what the world and the devil sends my way, I will always have God's grace to catapult me over my wall of fear and connect me to the unconditional love that conquers all.

What fears are you dealing with today? Take a moment to think about how those fears have kept you from sharing God's love with those in need. How often have those fears kept you from praying for a stranger, helping the homeless, loving the unlovable, reaching the lost, or giving hope to the hopeless? Think about how your wall of fear impacts your ability to share the love of Christ.

NO FEAR

Let's take a look at a passage in Hebrews that speaks so relevantly to our fears.

> Don't love money; be satisfied with what you have. For God has said, "I will never fail you. I will never abandon you."
> So we can say with confidence, "The LORD is my helper, so I will have no fear. What can mere people do to me?" – Hebrews 13:5–6

Quoting Deuteronomy 31:6 and Psalm 118:6–7, the author of Hebrews shows that God has promised He will never fail us or abandon us; He gives us the confidence to boast in the Lord and to have no fear.

And right after this, the writer adds:

> Remember your leaders who taught you the word of God. Think of all the good that has come from their lives, and follow the example of their faith.
> – Hebrews 13:7

This verse serves as a reminder of how important it is for others to be able to look back on our legacy someday and know that much good came from our lives because we conquered our walls of fear and spread the gospel with our testimony. Satan's main motivation for bringing fearful times your way is to keep you from connecting with the love of God and sharing the message of Christ. He wants your wall of fear to stay fortified so that the kingdom doesn't grow through your life.

For me, the year 2009 was filled with both great opportunities and strategic attacks from the enemy to keep me from fulfilling my calling. In addition to having a speaking ministry with wonderful opportunities, I am now planting a church, yet Satan attacks me with fear every day. But what I recognize now that I didn't see as clearly in 2009 is that on the other side of conquering my wall of fear are occasions to share the message of Jesus in a powerful way.

For me it's worth the fight. The spiritual success that awaits me is worth taking a sledgehammer to my wall of shadowy darkness. I promise that it will be worth it for you to demolish your wall of fear as well.

And by the way . . . after a stem-cell transplant, my dad's cancer is in remission; subsequent checkups and blood work revealed that my wife didn't have cancer; after a couple of years of rehab, my mom is walking again; and after breaking my hand and arm, I finished my section of the Baja 1000.

You can take God's promise in Hebrews 13:5 to the bank: "I will never fail you. I will never abandon you."

FREE AT LAST

Now you are no longer a slave but God's own child. And since you are his child, God has made you his heir.

– Galatians 4:7

CHAPTER 7

A WALL OF ADDICTION

Freedom is a powerful thing.

The quest for freedom prompted President Abraham Lincoln to take a stand as our nation split and brother fought against brother during the Civil War. The quest for racial equality and freedom led Martin Luther King Jr. to cry out these words from an old slave spiritual: "Free at last! Free at last! Thank God Almighty, we are free at last!" The quest for freedom caused hundreds of thousands to celebrate with tears and cheers when the first chunk of the Berlin Wall fell. Throughout history we have learned that freedom is worth dying for.

CREATED FOR FREEDOM

Lightning bugs intrigued me when I was a kid. I used to sit on our back porch and watch them for hours. I would leap into action, catching as many as I could with a jar. I remember, though, how the thrill of capturing these amazing insects was diminished when I realized they would never light up once inside the jar. I could blow on them, shake the jar, throw some grass in there and hope a full stomach would provoke that bright spark of green light— but nothing would ever work. As soon as the lightning bugs were released, however, they would begin to light up again. I soon realized that freedom is what caused them to light up, so I stopped capturing them.

Let me share another example of the fact that to be robbed of freedom is to be robbed of the very thing for which we were created. I remember visiting SeaWorld as a child, on more than one occasion, and asking my mom why the fins on the whales drooped. Each time she told me it was because they were sad.

I never realized what that meant until years later when I traveled to South Africa with Athletes in Action to play some baseball and witness to folks there about Christ. I had a chance to head to the shores of Cape Town during whale-mating season, the time of year when these giant creatures come within a hundred yards of shore for all to see. What an amazing sight to watch the whales leaping out of the waves and spitting water out of their spouts, jumping and splashing as if they were kids at play. Unlike the whales I saw as a child at SeaWorld, their fins were straight up in the air. And they weren't responding to the commands of a trainer but rather to the sounds and feel of the wild—as if they were dancing with one another to a chorus of beautiful music.

Since that moment I have never been a big fan of zoos or theme parks that keep animals in captivity. Why? Because it robs them of their created purpose. What I saw that day on the shores of Cape Town, South Africa was the look of freedom—freedom that screams out purpose.

Now I'm not going to become a vegetarian or join PETA (People for the Ethical Treatment of Animals), but my point is that when freedom is not established in any created thing, you can tell it. And wouldn't that be even more true when it comes to God's greatest creation—the human race? I believe we were created to soar on eagles' wings, to run with unshackled chains, and to dream dreams that come to pass. What I see in many people, however, are clipped wings, chained ankles, and nightmares that disrupt peaceful sleep. That absence of freedom, that slavery, is a wall that Satan wants to keep high, thick, strong, and fortified in our lives.

SLAVES OF CHRIST

The apostle Paul knew something about slavery and freedom. He went from literally imprisoning Christians for their beliefs to becoming "a slave of Christ Jesus" (Romans 1:1) and suffering for Him. Take a look at his resume of suffering recorded in 2 Corinthians 11:21–28:

> But whatever [the false apostles] dare to boast about—
> I'm talking like a fool again—I dare to boast about it,
> too. Are they Hebrews? So am I. Are they Israelites? So
> am I. Are they descendants of Abraham? So am I. Are
> they servants of Christ? I know I sound like a mad-
> man, but I have served him far more! I have worked
> harder, been put in prison more often, been whipped
> times without number, and faced death again and
> again. Five different times the Jewish leaders gave me

thirty-nine lashes. Three times I was beaten with rods. Once I was stoned. Three times I was shipwrecked. Once I spent a whole night and a day adrift at sea. I have traveled on many long journeys. I have faced danger from rivers and from robbers. I have faced danger from my own people, the Jews, as well as from the Gentiles. I have faced danger in the cities, in the deserts, and on the seas. And I have faced danger from men who claim to be believers but are not. I have worked hard and long, enduring many sleepless nights. I have been hungry and thirsty and have often gone without food. I have shivered in the cold, without enough clothing to keep me warm.

Then, besides all this, I have the daily burden of my concern for all the churches.

Paul never would have been able to go through this type of abuse had he not been "a slave of Christ Jesus," since that is what brings about true freedom. Jesus said, "You are truly my disciples if you remain faithful to my teachings. And you will know the truth, and the truth will set you free" (John 8:31–32).

As a follower of Christ, Paul suffered at a level which I doubt you or I could understand. He had a clear understanding of what freedom and slavery are all about, as we see in Galatians 4:1–7:

Think of it this way. If a father dies and leaves an inheritance for his young children, those children are not much better off than slaves until they grow up, even though they actually own everything their father had. They have to obey their guardians until they reach whatever age their father set. And that's the way it was with us before Christ came. We were like children; we were slaves to the basic spiritual principles of this world.

But when the right time came, God sent his Son, born of a woman, subject to the law. God sent him to buy freedom for us who were slaves to the law, so that he could adopt us as his very own children. And because we are his children, God has sent the Spirit of his Son into our hearts, prompting us to call out, "Abba, Father." Now you are no longer a slave but God's own child. And since you are his child, God has made you his heir.

A Day at the Salon

Jesus would often explain or illustrate a point by telling a story, and I would like to illustrate the point I am trying to make by telling a story as well. I believe something that happened to me several years ago will help you understand what Paul was communicating.

I had just come home, the night before, from a long and exhausting week of traveling and speaking. I woke up that morning looking forward to a day of rest and relaxation. But then my wife walked in the room and asked me a question she had never asked me before: "Christian, would you like to go to Becky's Hair Salon with me for the day?"

Maybe I was in a daze from the past week of ministry, but for some reason I said yes. As soon as that little three-letter word came out of my mouth, I asked myself, *What did you just say?*

But it was too late. My response evoked excitement in Amy's heart, and I was locked in to the deal for the rest of the day. So off I went, with my Bible in hand, riding shotgun in Amy's Honda

Odyssey as we headed to Kannapolis, North Carolina to hang out at Becky's for the day.

Now I went to school with Becky years ago and have been friends with her and her husband for a long time. Her shop, however, was always full of both women keeping up with the local gossip and with the smell of hair color and perfume—not a place in which a man would have a longing in his heart to hang out. But there I was.

When we pulled up, Amy asked me if I was coming in right away. I replied that I would sit in the car and read my Bible for a little while and then pop in and say hi. After reading my Bible a while, I began to focus in prayer on some upcoming speaking events. During that time, I clearly sensed God leading me to get out of the car and start walking. It was almost as if I was having an experience like Philip in Acts 8—when the Holy Spirit led him to run up to a chariot and wait for an opportunity to preach the gospel.

WALKING DOWN A COUNTRY ROAD

I have to admit that my first response was to question why God would have me get out of the car and walk down an old country road on a hot summer day. The name of the road is Old Beatty Ford Road, and I would imagine that the only traffic this road typically sees are the cars driven by women heading to Becky's for a day at the salon.

However, the voice of God was so real and the pull on my heart to be obedient was so strong that I stopped questioning, grabbed my Bible, and began to walk down the road. It turned out to be a beautiful day for walking, and I enjoyed taking in all the sights and sounds of being in the country. I watched the tree branches blow back and forth as a gentle wind made its way through the woods, and I noticed the beautiful wildflowers that were growing in an open field. I stopped on the side of the road to lean across a barbed-wire fence and talk to several cows that had made their way to find greener pastures to munch on there.

After I had walked a considerable distance, I noticed a van coming toward me. As the van passed by, a young woman stuck her head out the window and yelled, "What's up, baby?!" Now I have a mirror at my house, so I am very aware that God must have been at work here, because under no circumstances do I deserve a shout-out! I just ignored the girl and kept walking, until I noticed that the van had turned around and was making its way back toward me.

When the vehicle pulled up beside me, two girls leaned their heads out of the windows and tried to talk me into hopping in for a ride. One girl assured me I would be safe. When I declined, the other girl said it was way too hot and I was way too good-looking to be walking down the road by myself. Contending that I needed some company and some free air conditioning, she urged me to reconsider. I assured them that I was fine—I was a married man and would not be getting in their van.

They drove off and I assumed the adventure was over—until I saw that they had pulled into a driveway several hundred yards ahead. As I got closer, I could tell the girls were putting makeup on their faces while they were waiting for me. When I got next to the van, they got out; and I have to say that both girls were beautiful.

A DIVINE APPOINTMENT

This stroll down Old Beatty Ford Road suddenly reminded me of how Jesus was tempted by Satan in the wilderness just before He began His public ministry. I tried to prepare myself for battle, but I never could have imagined what God was about to do. As the girls approached me on the side of the road, I asked them why they were trying to pick up some man they had never met. "The world is way too sick and twisted to be trusting strangers on the side of a country road, even in the middle of the day," I informed them.

One of the girls then said that the reason they were there was because her sister had died in a head-on collision on that road ten years earlier, and she had come to replace the flowers at the side of the road where her sister had passed away.

"What was your sister's name?" I asked.

"Haley," the girl replied.

"Was your sister married to a guy named Chris?" I then asked.

She turned pale white, remembering that I had preached at her sister's memorial service.

"Your sister's husband is related to my wife, and we knew Chris and Haley quite well," I said. "I remember you from ten years ago, when you were just a young girl."

She then broke down in tears, telling me that she had been partying with her friend for twenty-four hours straight—smoking weed, drinking, and taking pain pills. She also told me that since I had last seen her, ten years ago, she had gotten pregnant and had a baby but gave the child to her family to raise because of her way of life. She added that her grandfather was a pastor and that her family was very disappointed in her lifestyle choices. She said she knew that people were praying nonstop for her as she was trying to figure out this thing called life.

I then shared with her how my day started and what led me to the point where we were now face-to-face—how I had never gone to Becky's with my wife before and how the Lord had spoken to me in the car and directed me to take my Bible and just start walking down that country road.

"Do you think it was a coincidence that I would be walking down this road at the very same time that you were driving down this road to replace the flowers at the place where your sister lost her life ten years ago?" I asked. "And could it have been a coincidence that I was the one who preached the memorial service for your sister, and I remember you sitting on the front row of the church crying when you were just a young teenager?"

I tried to help her see how God had orchestrated this occasion for us to meet so she would have an opportunity to repent of her sins and switch from slavery to freedom. I pointed out that drinking, drugs, and wild living had put her in chains and was preventing her from being the person God had called her to be. I explained to her what true freedom is and how that freedom can only be found in a personal relationship with Jesus Christ.

When I asked her if she wanted to repent of her sins and give her life to Jesus, she said yes. As we called out to the Lord together along the side of the road, this girl made a decision to follow Christ and be transformed from a child of slavery to a child of God—set free in Christ.

If the apostle Paul had been there with us, I'm sure he would have declared to this young woman, in the spirit of Galatians 4:6–7, "Because you are his child, God has sent the Spirit of his Son into your heart, prompting you to call out, 'Abba Father.' Now you are no longer a slave but God's own child. And since you are his child, God has made you his heir."

As evidence of her sincere repentance, she handed me a bag full of marijuana and pills and asked me to get rid of them for her.

Sometimes I wonder what happened to the young lady who received Christ on the side of Old Beatty Ford Road. Is she still walking in freedom? Or has she allowed the world to put her back in chains?

I do know what happened to the other girl I met that day. When I asked her if she would like to pray with us and invite Jesus into her life, she responded, "No, I'm fine with things the way they are." She was a Carolina Panther cheerleader at the time, and we became "friends" on Facebook. From time to time I would notice her posts, the nature of which led me to believe she was still living a life of slavery to the world. Eventually she wrote on her Facebook page that her boyfriend had beaten her so badly that she had to be admitted to the hospital, and that she was going to move to another state and go into hiding. She held on to her wall of addiction that stemmed from alcohol and drugs.

WHAT ARE YOUR WALLS?

The crux of this chapter, to be honest, is to not let you off the hook. I want to force you to identify any walls of addiction you might have in your life that supersede your commitment to Christ.

- Does alcohol or drugs consume you?
- Does an addiction to pornography or some other form of lust keep you chained?
- What about an activity that isn't wrong in and of itself— like eating, shopping, or watching TV—but you have let it control you rather than you controlling it?
- Are you in a relationship that is unhealthy, holding onto it even though you know you should bail out?
- Are you enslaved to the love of money and the desire for more?

Paul rebuked the new believers in Galatia for allowing something to supersede their commitment to Christ.

Oh, foolish Galatians! Who has cast an evil spell on you? For the meaning of Jesus Christ's death was made as clear to you as if you had seen a picture of his death on the cross. Let me ask you this one question: Did you receive the Holy Spirit by obeying the law of Moses? Of course not! You received the Spirit because you believed the message you heard about Christ. How foolish can you be? After starting your Christian lives in the Spirit, why are you now trying to become perfect by your own human effort? – Galatians 3:1–3

The Galatians were addicted, in a sense, to following the customs of the Jewish law, which made them feel safe and secure. They were addicted to their attempts to earn their right standing with God through their own efforts. Paul challenged the Christians in Galatia by making them look at where they had come from in their past and where they were currently heading in their spiritual lives.

And that is how I want to challenge you as we conclude this chapter. Consider your life—your past, your present, and your future. What chains from your past bind and haunt you? What challenges keep you living in fear in the present? What bondages will prevent you from being free in the future?

Prison walls are built to keep guilty people from experiencing freedom. Satan tries to maintain and reinforce these walls of slavery. But you have been bought with a price—and that price was paid so you could be free from your sin and guilt.

"Free at last! Free at last! Thank God Almighty, we are free at last!"

Are you free?

Religion versus Relationship

A person is a fool to store up
earthly wealth but not have a rich
relationship with God.

– Luke 12:21

CHAPTER 8

A WALL OF RELIGION

Do you have "a rich relationship with God," using Jesus' words in Luke 12:21, or do you have a religion that goes no deeper than attending a worship service once a week? That's a stiff opening question, for sure, but a valid question—a question that needs to be asked because religion brings death and relationship brings life.

Now I know your initial reaction might be something like this: "Bro, I was baptized at youth camp when I was thirteen, I have a Christian bumper sticker on my car, a cross necklace around my neck, a tattoo of the fish symbol on my wrist, a Bible on my coffee table, I attend church every Sunday, and I tithe 10 percent of every paycheck (and have the tax write-off to prove it)."

Well, if that—or anything close to that—was your first thought, then you need to read this chapter twice!

For this topic I am using the following definitions from Dictionary.com:

Religion: A set of beliefs concerning the cause, nature, and purpose of the universe, especially when considered as the creation of a superhuman agency or agencies, usually involving devotional and ritual observances.

Relationship: An emotional connection, or other connection, between people.

WHICH ONE PLEASES GOD?

Which of the two describe your spiritual life? And which do you think God desires more—a set of beliefs and the expression of your faith through ritual observances, or a connection between you and Himself? I think the Scriptures are pretty clear about the answer to that question. Take a look, for example, at a couple of statements Paul made in his letter to the Romans:

> Clearly, God's promise to give the whole earth to Abraham and his descendants was based not on his obedience to God's law, but on a right relationship with God that comes by faith. – Romans 4:13

> Since our friendship with God was restored by the death of his Son while we were still his enemies, we will certainly be saved through the life of his Son. So now we can rejoice in our wonderful new relationship with God because our Lord Jesus Christ has made us friends of God. – Romans 5:10–11

A relationship is what God desires the most. More than our beliefs, traditions, and rituals, God wants our passion and joy to be for Him and in Him. According to James 2:19, even the demons believe in the one true God. Traditions don't necessarily keep us connected to God, but rather tend to wane in connectivity in our ever-changing world. And every religion has rituals.

Only a relationship with God produces a pure spiritual passion and true joy. Satan might rob us of our happiness, but he can never steal our godly passion and joy. Nothing is more powerful than to connect with and serve the God who hung the stars.

NICK AT NIGHT

If you're having trouble seeing the difference between religion and relationship, don't feel bad. After encountering Jesus, an astute Jewish religious leader named Nicodemus was a little lost on the subject. Nicodemus would find out what really matters when it comes to heaven and spiritual things.

Let's take a look at their conversation.

> There was a man named Nicodemus, a Jewish religious leader who was a Pharisee. After dark one evening, he came to speak with Jesus. "Rabbi," he said, "we all know that God has sent you to teach us. Your miraculous signs are evidence that God is with you."
>
> Jesus replied, "I tell you the truth, unless you are born again, you cannot see the Kingdom of God."
>
> "What do you mean?" exclaimed Nicodemus. "How can an old man go back into his mother's womb and be born again?"

Jesus replied, "I assure you, no one can enter the Kingdom of God without being born of water and the Spirit. Humans can reproduce only human life, but the Holy Spirit gives birth to spiritual life. So don't be surprised when I say, 'You must be born again.' The wind blows wherever it wants. Just as you can hear the wind but can't tell where it comes from or where it is going, so you can't explain how people are born of the Spirit."

"How are these things possible?" Nicodemus asked.

Jesus replied, "You are a respected Jewish teacher, and yet you don't understand these things? I assure you, we tell you what we know and have seen, and yet you won't believe our testimony. But if you don't believe me when I tell you about earthly things, how can you possibly believe if I tell you about heavenly things? No one has ever gone to heaven and returned. But the Son of Man has come down from heaven. And as Moses lifted up the bronze snake on a pole in the wilderness, so the Son of Man must be lifted up, so that everyone who believes in him will have eternal life.

"For God loved the world so much that he gave his one and only Son, so that everyone who believes in him will not perish but have eternal life."
– John 3:1–16

Jesus was trying to explain to Nicodemus that God is looking for relationship. Nicodemus couldn't understand that because his whole life had been wrapped up in religion. Nicodemus was a member of the Jewish sect called the Pharisees—which means "the separated ones"—and the Sanhedrin, the prestigious Jewish ruling council. But even though Nicodemus represented the epitome of religious zeal and commitment, he was hungry for more. That is always the case with religion, because it always leaves you feeling empty and craving for more.

Nicodemus came to Jesus at night, probably because he didn't want to be seen with Him, and engaged Jesus in conversation. When Nicodemus didn't understand Jesus' statements about being "born again," he asked Jesus some direct and honest questions. Jesus must have had a read on Nicodemus's heart, given the way He confronted Nicodemus's ignorance: "You are a respected Jewish teacher, and yet you don't understand these things? I assure you, we tell you what we know and have seen, and yet you won't believe our testimony. But if you don't believe me when I tell you about earthly things, how can you possibly believe if I tell you about heavenly things?"

RELIGION'S EFFECTS

Jesus' words indicate that Nicodemus's religion had caused him to be blind to the truth that could set him free. That's what a wall of religion does. It affects our spiritual senses and keeps us from obtaining the relationship that seals the deal. It keeps us from seeing, hearing, and experiencing the things of God. And as long as the wall stands, we are blocked from connecting to God through a relationship with His Son.

Having a relationship with Christ, as opposed to going through the motions of a religion dictated by rules and rituals, makes a profound difference in a person's life. For example . . .

- Religion says, "Go to church one day a week." Relationship says, "I get to worship God seven days a week."

- Religion says, "Read your Bible every day, so your checklist is complete." Relationship says, "Study the Word of God and live it out."
- Religion says, "It has to be done this way." Relationship says, "However You lead me, Lord, I will follow."
- Religion says, "My wife and children have to respect me and submit to me, because I am the man of the house and because the Bible says so." Relationship says, "I will spend quality time with my wife and children, and then respect and submission will follow."
- Religion says, "It's all about rules." Relationship says, "It's all about love."
- Religion says, "They must be punished." Relationship says, "They must be forgiven."

I could go on, but I think you get my point.

Growing Up with A Wall

To be honest, I feel like an expert on this subject due to the fact that I have experienced both religion and relationship and know how it feels to be on both sides. I grew up in the small city of Kannapolis, North Carolina. If you're into towels and bed linens or NASCAR racing, you might be familiar with this town. But unfortunately the mammoth Cannon Mills textile plant shut down years ago; and Dale Earnhardt Sr., who was born and raised in Kannapolis, was killed—doing what he loved—in a crash at Turn 4 at the Daytona 500 in 2001. About all that's left in Kannapolis are some old mill houses, vacant stores and restaurants, and hundred-year-old churches that are just barely hanging on.

The church I grew up in is located near downtown, and my mind is filled with childhood memories of growing up in a traditional church in the small-town South. Though I love the church and the people in Kannapolis today, many of the memories I have of growing up there aren't memories of relationship and love but rather of religious tension and regret.

I remember playing behind the church after youth group on Wednesdays and being told never to cross the gully behind the church because dangerous black people lived in the apartment complex back there. I vividly recall one day after youth group when I was standing at that gully, holding a basketball, and some black kids on the other side of the gully were holding their basketballs. We looked at each other, not knowing what to say. My heart was filled with hurt and confusion and I'm sure they felt the same way, as we were unable to understand why both sides wouldn't allow a connection.

Later on, when I was in my early teens, I helped out at the church sometimes and wondered why there was always a van with tinted windows parked behind the church. I finally asked the pastor who the van belonged to, and he said it belonged to the police department. The church was allowing them to park in the back parking lot and film "illegal activities" taking place in the apartment complex. I remember the frustration I felt, even as a youngster, that the church would agree to help set those folks up to go to jail but wouldn't welcome them into the sanctuary so they could hear the message of freedom in Christ.

I remember when my cousin, back in the 80s, let his hair grow really long and was asked to quit singing in the choir because he was "a bad example." Some of my relatives got so mad that they left the church.

I remember getting a new worship leader who convinced the leadership to start the Sunday service fifteen minutes earlier, at

10:45 instead of 11:00, so that we could mix in some contemporary music with the standard repertoire—and hopefully connect
with all generations and ages. So many people complained that
a meeting was held after church one Sunday, and the congregation voted to start at 11:00 again and not to allow contemporary
music in the worship service. It wasn't long before that young
worship leader, his heart crushed, resigned and went to another church.

One time back in the 90s, during the days that DC Talk first
became popular, I remember the youth pastor playing some of
their music through the brand-new sound system in the sanctuary
when an elder of the church walked in; he said he had given a lot of
money to buy that sound system and he was *not* going to let music
inspired by the devil be played through it.

I remember occasions when the church planned to vote on
whether or not to keep the pastor, and people who had left the
church would start making calls to rally support for their cause to
get rid of the pastor and then show up on Sunday to cast a vote
that I felt they had no right to cast. One pastor who got voted
out sarcastically stated that he always enjoyed voting Sunday because the church would be full, since people he hadn't seen in years
would always come out to vote.

Now it's only fair to say that there were good times as well. And
I have no doubt that many of the older saints in the church prayed
me right out of hell during my teen years when I was a drug addict
and a drunk. But we typically remember the bad things the most,
and I think it would be accurate to say that the things I remember
the most are the scars and wounds associated with religion.

THE WALL TAKES A BLOW

Several years ago I was excited to hear that my old church in Kannapolis was getting a new pastor, a young Northerner named James who had a flare for contemporary worship. I decided to give James a call and encourage him in his new endeavor for the Lord. I challenged him to stay focused on his calling through thick and thin, warning him that he might have to fight some battles to get to the good stuff God had down the road. James thanked me for my concern but assured me he would be fine. I told him to feel free to call me because he would probably need to talk at some point.

Not too long after that I was at a get-together with some members of my family who still attend the church, so I asked them how the new pastor was doing. Their response was that he was way too radical for the church and probably wouldn't be there very long. For one thing, he had plowed up some land next to the church that wasn't being used so that he could plant a garden and take the produce to the government-housing neighborhood behind the church—the neighborhood I was excluded from as a child.

They also reported that James was going to questionable parts of town and inviting people to church who really shouldn't be there, and that he was preaching too long and going past the allotted time—which is from 11:00 to 12:00 and no later. They grumbled that the youth pastor James brought in to serve with him had long hair and a tattoo. Although the youth group had grown from twenty to sixty-five kids, it was unacceptable to have a hoodlum leading them.

When I heard all this, I got really excited. James definitely sounded like my kind of guy! So I decided to call him again and share some words of affirmation. After we talked a while, I could tell he was very frustrated and wounded because of what he had experienced in the short amount of time he had been in Kannapolis. I encouraged him to hang on, saying that the people have good hearts but just needed to be trained on the importance of relationship instead of religion.

I'm glad to say that James decided to dig in and stick it out, and today the church is growing in leaps and bounds both numerically and in terms of having a relationship with Jesus. A younger group of people is coming and mixing together in a healthy way with the older generation. The worship services blend contemporary music with traditional music. And sometimes they even get out at 12:15 instead of 12:00!

After several phone conversations, James and I became good friends. Wanting to see his passion for the Lord spill over into the lives of those I love, I have prayed for James and encouraged him often. I recently attended the church's homecoming service, and it was dramatically different than what I remembered as a kid. The church has made a drastic turn from being religious to being relational, and the effects are being seen and heard all over Kannapolis.

The best news of all is that some of the people who live behind the church are feeling welcome enough to come. That's the power of what a relationship with Christ can bring. Religion will get you nowhere, but relationship will take you all the way to your eternal resting place in heaven.

BACK TO NICODEMUS

Well, that's a good ending to a story that had a rough start. But what about Nicodemus and his story—would he make the transition from religion to relationship? We can find out by looking at the two other passages in the New Testament in which he appears.

The instance in which Nicodemus approached Jesus to speak with Him at night occurred early in Jesus' ministry. A couple of years later Jesus returned to Jerusalem for the Festival of Tabernacles, and He and His teaching were met with strong opposition from the Jewish religious leaders.

With the Holy City packed with pilgrims, Jesus made a profoundly "relational" statement: "On the last day, the climax of the festival, Jesus stood and shouted to the crowds, 'Anyone who is thirsty may come to me! Anyone who believes in me may come and drink! For the Scriptures declare, "Rivers of living water will flow from his heart"'" (John 7:37–38).

Filled with jealousy and disdain, the leadership of the Sanhedrin sent the Temple guards to arrest Jesus. But now the plot thickens, as Nicodemus reenters the stage.

> When the Temple guards returned without having arrested Jesus, the leading priests and Pharisees demanded, "Why didn't you bring him in?"
>
> "We have never heard anyone speak like this!" the guards responded.
>
> "Have you been led astray, too?" the Pharisees mocked. "Is there a single one of us rulers or Pharisees who believes in him? This foolish crowd follows him, but they are ignorant of the law. God's curse is on them!"
>
> Then Nicodemus, the leader who had met with Jesus earlier, spoke up. "Is it legal to convict a man before he is given a hearing?" he asked.
>
> They replied, "Are you from Galilee, too? Search the Scriptures and see for yourself—no prophet ever comes from Galilee!" – John 7:45–52

Here we see the Jewish religious leaders in full rage over the testimony of Jesus, criticizing all those who speak out on His behalf. With the veins in their necks popping out, no doubt, they shout that only those who have no knowledge of Scripture are getting excited about Jesus' claims. So for Nicodemus, whom Jesus Himself called "a respected Jewish teacher" in John 3:10, to speak out on behalf of Jesus was a bold move. Laying his status as a prominent religious leader on the line, Nicodemus's wall of religion was clearly starting to come down.

Our final encounter with Nicodemus in the New Testament, which occurs soon after Jesus takes His last breath on the cross, is nothing short of a show-stopper.

> Joseph of Arimathea, who had been a secret disciple of Jesus (because he feared the Jewish leaders), asked Pilate for permission to take down Jesus' body. When Pilate gave permission, Joseph came and took the body away. With him came Nicodemus, the man who had come to Jesus at night. He brought about seventy-five pounds of perfumed ointment made from myrrh and aloes. Following Jewish burial custom, they wrapped Jesus' body with the spices in long sheets of linen cloth. The place of crucifixion was near a garden, where there was a new tomb, never used before. And so, because it was the day of preparation for the Jewish Passover and since the tomb was close at hand, they laid Jesus there. – John 19:38–42

Isn't it interesting that both men had been afraid to live out their faith openly but now are asking for Jesus' body so that they can provide a proper Jewish burial for this man who had been condemned to death? We can see that a wall of religion had fallen in their lives, as they went from being clandestine followers of Jesus to being willing to be harassed for His sake. Yes, a wall of religion had definitely come down.

HIT AWAY!

What about you? Does your faith go no deeper than a Sunday morning experience? When you fall on hard times, do you reach out for religion or do you cry out for Jesus? Let me urge you to confront and bring down any religious wall. Don't allow yourself to get stuck in a dead routine of tradition. Instead, come to life with a passionate relationship with Jesus.

In the classic baseball movie *The Natural*, the crooked principal owner of the 1939 New York Knights tries to pressure baseball's new sensation, Roy Hobbs (Robert Redford), not to play in the team's one-game playoff for the National League pennant, since losing the game would give him full control of the team. When Hobbs is asked, before the championship-deciding game, what he plans to do, he replies, "Hit away."

When it comes to tearing down any and all walls in your life, I would encourage you to do the same: Hit away!

I BELIEVE

Jesus said to the disciples, "Have faith in God. I tell you the truth, you can say to this mountain, 'May you be lifted up and thrown into the sea,' and it will happen. But you must really believe it will happen and have no doubt in your heart."

— Mark 11:22–23

CHAPTER 9

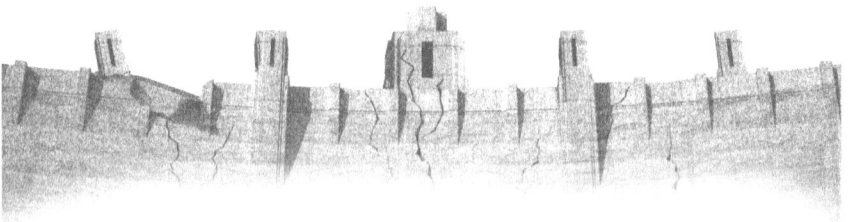

A WALL OF DOUBT

Several years ago I watched the *Larry King Live* show as Larry King interviewed one of my heroes in the faith, Billy Graham. They discussed Rev. Graham's final crusade and what it meant to him to serve the Lord for well over fifty years and to reach millions of people around the world.

Hanging on Rev. Graham's every word, as I always do, I heard something quite unexpected. When Larry King asked him if he ever had doubts about what he was preaching, Rev. Graham replied, "Yes, I have had doubts."

What?! Billy Graham has had doubts?! He went on to say that he had dealt with many days of doubt, but that the many days of confirmation from the Lord had helped him to continue the good fight and finish the race for Christ.

Likewise, when Mother Teresa wrote her private letters near the end of her life, she shared about her agonizing doubts. C. S. Lewis struggled with doubt when his beloved wife was stricken with cancer and died. Abraham Lincoln struggled with doubt, especially when the Civil War started to tip in the Confederates' favor.

These are the same kind of doubts that a man I met recently who just lost his four-year-old daughter to leukemia faces. These are the same kind of doubts that a wife and mother who recently heard me speak faces. In the e-mail she sent to me, she stated that she had never felt so on fire for Jesus. "But how will I keep that passion when Monday's struggles come around?" she asked.

It's a common conflict, this wall of doubt that we all confront as we strive to keep our faith firm in a world straying further and further from the truth. A wall of doubt can keep us from fulfilling God's plan for our lives. The battle to tear down this wall is definitely worth fighting.

ANTIDOTES TO DOUBT

There are many ways to approach this wall. From a statistical perspective, I could recount something I've heard Josh McDowell, the well-known Christian apologist, mention. The odds of Jesus fulfilling all the prophecies about the Messiah in the Old Testament are equivalent to someone filling up the entire state of Texas two feet deep in silver dollars and throwing a gold coin somewhere in the pile—and then having someone jump out of a plane, open their parachute, float gently to earth, and land directly on that one gold coin.

From an archaeological standpoint, I could focus on the discoveries that have led people to affirm the accuracy of the Bible. For instance, when Sodom and Gomorrah were discovered there was ash everywhere—telling archaeologists that the cities were completely destroyed by fire, just as Genesis 19 states.

We could talk about the Dead Sea Scrolls, ancient scrolls that predate Jesus by one or two centuries. Hidden away in the rocky caves near the Dead Sea, the first scrolls were discovered in 1947 by a Bedouin shepherd boy looking for a lost lamb. Considered to be the greatest archaeological discovery of the twentieth century, if not of all time, the Dead Sea Scrolls include copies of Old Testament Hebrew texts that are about a thousand years closer to the original writings than were previously known—clearly demonstrating the authenticity and reliability of the Old Testament. Of particular note is a large, twenty-four-foot long complete copy of the book of Isaiah. Scholars concur that the "Great Isaiah Scroll" is virtually identical to later Isaiah texts, the oldest of which was produced about 1100 years later.

And a comparison of the more than 5,700 Greek New Testament manuscripts—hand copied over a span of hundreds of years—that have been discovered, reveals no significant differences. God has clearly protected the transmission of His Word through the ages.

I could share reports about how divers several years ago were searching for evidence of the Israelites miraculously crossing the Red Sea when they came across chariot wheels, spears, and human and horse remains on the floor of the Red Sea. They found this crossing site because of a pillar, discovered at the edge of the water, that marked the spot where the crossing took place and dates back to the time of Solomon three thousand years ago. Chariot wheels, covered in coral, were dislodged from the chariots—confirming the biblical account in Exodus 14:25:

> Just before dawn the LORD looked down on the Egyptian army from the pillar of fire and cloud, and he threw their forces into total confusion. He twisted [or removed] their chariot wheels, making their

chariots difficult to drive. "Let's get out of here—away from these Israelites!" the Egyptians shouted. "The LORD is fighting for them against Egypt!"

From the world of science, I could share about the many occasions in which scientists have been proven wrong and therefore changed their theories on the origin of life—yet they want us to trust them today.

Here's an interesting quote from George Wald, who taught at Harvard and won a share of the 1967 Noble Prize in Physiology or Medicine:

> When it comes to the origin of life, we have only two possibilities as to how life arose. One is spontaneous generation arising to evolution; the other is a supernatural creative act of God. There is no third possibility. . . . Spontaneous generation was scientifically disproved one hundred years ago by Louis Pasteur, Spellanzani, Reddy and others. That leads us scientifically to only one possible conclusion—that life arose as a supernatural creative act of God. . . . I will not accept that philosophically because I do not want to believe in God. Therefore, I choose to believe in that which I know is scientifically impossible, spontaneous generation arising to evolution. (*Scientific American*, August, 1954)

The professor doesn't sound very confident, does he?

One of the world's current leaders in evolution is Richard Dawkins, professor emeritus at Oxford. When he was interviewed by Ben Stein as part of the 2008 documentary film *Expelled: No Intelligence Allowed*, his response was nothing short of amazing:

It could be that at some earlier time, somewhere in the universe, a civilization evolved, probably by some kind of Darwinian means, probably to a very high level of technology, and designed a form of life that they seeded onto perhaps this planet.

Wow—we might be descendants of aliens!

If science struggles to explain where life came from, it struggles just as much to explain where our craving for love and relationships comes from. As believers, we know that the Bible says that love comes from God and that our hunger for relationship is driven, first of all, by our desire to be connected with our Creator.

From the historical vantage point, we can note the written evidence that Jesus actually lived, died, and was resurrected from the dead. One of the most credible sources, aside from the New Testament, is the writings of the highly respected first-century Jewish historian Flavius Josephus. Though some scholars speculate that the following quote was inserted later by a Christian copyist, Josephus's *Jewish Antiquities*, first published in AD 93, includes this:

> Now there was about this time Jesus, a wise man, if it be lawful to call him a man; for he was a doer of wonderful works, a teacher of such men as receive the truth with pleasure. He drew over to him both many of the Jews and many of the Gentiles. He was [the] Christ. And when Pilate, at the suggestion of the principal men amongst us, had condemned him to the cross, those that loved him at the first did not forsake him; for he appeared to them alive again the third day; as the divine prophets had foretold these and ten thousand other wonderful things concerning

him. And the tribe of Christians, so named from him,
are not extinct at this day.

From the naturalist viewpoint, simply consider the following questions:

- Have you ever driven through the Great Smoky Mountains
  in the fall and looked at the leaves as they exploded with
  colors of red, orange, purple, and yellow?
- Have you ever walked outside at night to watch the lightning bugs fly or to gaze at the canopy of countless stars?
- Have you ever noticed how blue the sky is in Colorado
  or how green the grass is in the rolling hills of Kentucky?
- Have you ever watched the sun set over the desert plains
  of Arizona or stood on the beaches of South Carolina and
  watched the sun rise?
- Have you ever walked in the woods while snow was falling
  and felt the purity of a snowflake as it gently landed on
  your face?
- Have you ever sat on your front porch during a thun-
  derstorm and watched the landscape light up as lightning
  strikes spread across the dark sky?
- Have you ever paused on a hot summer day to enjoy the
  refreshment of a cool breeze?

How does anything but a loving and thoughtful Creator begin
to explain or justify any of these delights?

The Power of a God Story

Clearly there are many things that could bring down a wall of doubt. But let me assure you that nothing crumbles a wall of doubt like a God story. In my first book, *Testify*, I wrote at length about the power of a God story, or testimony, and how those stories strengthen our faith and prevent walls of doubt from being erected.

Let me share an awesome God story with you, one I heard from a special friend of mine. In addition to being a wonderful husband and father, Wade McHargue is a mighty servant of God. A career missionary, Wade and his family are currently ministering on an Indian reservation in South Dakota, living and serving in one of the poorest environments in the entire country. Alcoholism, drug addiction, divorce, disease, and death are at incredibly high levels.

Before Wade and his wife and children moved to this frozen tundra, I asked if I could take him out for lunch so that we could spend some time together. He happily agreed, so off we went to my favorite restaurant, Wild Wings Bar and Grill. I got a kick out of watching this 6'10" missionary eat wings for the first time in years. In between his many trips to the buffet counter, he shared about the work he and family had been doing in Africa and about their new calling to reach out to a lost and lonely Native American tribe in South Dakota.

Since God stories always seem to accompany missionaries, I asked Wade to share a story that would be an encouragement both to me and to others. Without hesitation, he began to tell me a story that I will never forget. During the three and a half years that Wade spent in Guinea-Bissau in West Africa, he saw God do many incredible things, but none was more powerful than what He did in a small hospital in a war-torn region of the country.

This hospital is basically run by the military, which is so corrupt that one of its generals is on America's most-wanted list. Because the hospital was filled with people dying of HIV/AIDS, Wade found himself on the front lines of ministry. This region is so populated with HIV/AIDS victims that medical experts believe the virus has mutated into a worse strain, causing people to die more quickly after contracting the disease. Wade felt called to go and pray regularly for the sick people in the hospital.

One day Wade prayed for a woman who weighed barely seventy pounds and, according to the medical staff, was only days away from dying. She couldn't eat, drink, or talk and was even having trouble breathing. Nevertheless, Wade laid his hands on her and then prayed and read Scriptures over her dying body. A week later, Wade felt impressed to return to the hospital and pray for the woman again. He was excited to find her sitting up in bed and able to talk and eat. Wade praised God for healing her, and then the woman gave her life to Christ!

The following week the woman was doing so well that she was released from the hospital. The medical staff acknowledged that a miracle of God clearly had blessed this woman who had been so sick. With their own eyes they had seen this skeleton of a person receive complete healing. This impacted not only their lives, but others as well. Wade and his team started to see more miraculous healings in the hospital.

One of the military officers saw his wife, who was so sick that she was near death's door, get healed. So he asked Wade what happened to her. Wade responded that the kingdom of heaven had come to the hospital and that God had healed his wife. Then this man, who was a Muslim, gave his life to Christ.

As miracle after miracle occurred in the hospital, the news quickly spread to the military base. That opened the door for Wade to begin giving out Bibles and praying for the soldiers. He even got an opportunity to share the gospel with the general who is on America's most-wanted list.

What a great story! And as I was reflecting on this story again while writing this chapter, I was prompted to call Wade and catch up with him. He reported that a revival had just broken out on the reservation in the past weekend. Eleven people gave their lives to Christ and twenty-five people were miraculously healed of various infirmities—including a woman who was healed of the effects of a stroke and a man who received sight after being blind for years!

How can science explain these stories? Science can only explain the natural, not the supernatural—which is why our God stories are so powerful.

FOSSILS OR FAITH?

This reminds me of a battle that nearly went down several months ago. It started when a biology professor at an Ivy League school saw an article about my hard stance on creationism. Since he was bringing a class to North Carolina to study the Appalachian Mountains, he challenged me to go to the top of the mountains with his class, where he assured me he would show fossils and soil samples that would disprove my Christian faith.

I made a deal with him that he could have as much time as he wanted as long as he would give me thirty minutes to share the gospel and my testimony with his class. He agreed, but as the time grew closer he started trying to back out, and eventually he just wanted to have a lunch meeting in Charlotte. Even though he wouldn't admit it, I knew why he didn't want to expose his class to the gospel. The story of Jesus' resurrection will always be more powerful than a bunch of fossils. My testimony of what God has done in my life will always be more powerful than soil samples, as amazing as I'm sure they are, from the Appalachian Mountains.

No doubt the professor and his biology class would have tried all day to convince me there is no God. But I also believe that when I shared all the things I have seen God do in my life, at the least the students would have been challenged, and perhaps their eyes would have been opened to the truth. You can't argue with faith fueled by the miracle of Christ's resurrection. There were so many things I wanted to share with that class: how God has loved me, how God has forgiven me, how God has healed me, how God has provided for me, how God has set me free, how God has broken down walls in my life.

Oh the power of a God story. Oh the power of a testimony to bring down a wall of doubt.

GOD STORIES IN THE BIBLE

The Israelites had a story to tell when their wall of doubt called the wall of Jericho fell down. Shadrach, Meshach, and Abednego had a story to tell when they walked through the fiery furnace without getting burned. Peter had a story to tell when he walked on top of a dark and deep lake.

Mary and Martha had a story to tell when Jesus and raised their dead brother from the dead. Martha had her doubts when Jesus told the people at Lazarus's tomb to push aside the large stone that had been rolled across the entrance of the tomb. But notice Jesus' promise of the power that can be released through our faith: "Didn't I tell you that you would see God's glory if you believe?" (John 11:40).

In Mark 11:22–23 Jesus said that our faith in God has the power to move mountains, and it would seem that our faith also has the power to see the dead raised back to life.

Think of the story Abraham could tell about raising a knife to slay his son Isaac when God provided a ram for the sacrifice just in the nick of time. Think of the story King David could tell about the day when he, though just a boy, brought down a nine-foot-tall Philistine champion with a rock and a sling. Think about the man who, possessed by a horde of demons, lived in rock-hewn tombs, night and day crying out and cutting himself with stones. Think of the story of hope he could tell about being set free by Jesus. Think of the story Paul could tell about how he hated and persecuted Christians—until he became one of them.

Think of all the stories the Israelites could tell around a camp-fire about God rescuing them from slavery so they could inherit a land flowing with milk and honey. Let's stop and reflect on that period of Israel's history for a moment because it provides such a fitting illustration of a wall of doubt. God's chosen people were miraculously liberated from bondage, ushered out of Egypt, escorted through the parted waters of the Red Sea, and given water from a rock and manna from heaven. Incredulously, though, after all of this they fashioned a golden calf and sank into idolatry. *How many miracles are enough?* is the obvious question.

I believe their doubts and lack of faith came from forgetting what God had done for them. Forgetting their God stories caused them to revert back to their default mentality of slavery, which is what a wall of doubt will do. Had they consciously focused on remembering the plagues God had sent to free them, the pillar of cloud and pillar of fire by which God had protected them, the Lord's miracle at the Red Sea which had not only given them safe passage but had destroyed Pharaoh's army, and God's provision of food and water in a desolate desert, they never would have desired to go back to Egypt.

YOUR PERSONAL PROMISED LAND

One consolation, at least, is that the Israelites proved that our own walls of doubt are nothing new. What promised land are you missing out on because you have forgotten your God stories? How much longer will you stay in slavery due to walls of doubt?

The odds of apologetics are in our favor. Archaeologists have dug up convincing evidence. The attempts of modern science to deny our faith have failed. Our longing for love and relationship points to God. History records too much about Jesus for that written testimony to be wrong. And creation declares the reality of the Creator.

But oh the power of a story. Not just mine, but yours. We're surrounded by stories that confirm our faith and tear down our walls of doubt.

What have you forgotten that you need to remember?

I think I just saw a wall start crashing down!

OH NO, HE DIDN'T!

He had to go through Samaria on
the way. Eventually he came to the
Samaritan village of Sychar, near
the field that Jacob gave to his son
Joseph. Jacob's well was there; and
Jesus, tired from the long walk,
sat wearily beside the well about
noontime. Soon a Samaritan woman
came to draw water, and Jesus said
to her, "Please give me a drink."

– John 4:4–7

CHAPTER 10

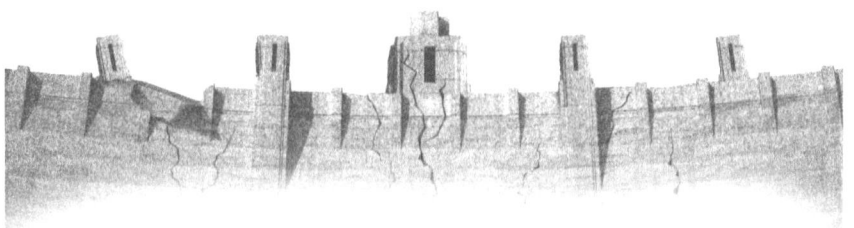

A WALL OF RACISM

I love the story of Jesus and the woman at the well. It's definitely one of my favorite stories to preach, and all the amazing things taking place in this brief passage make it a powerhouse when it comes to tearing down walls. For Jesus to talk with a Samaritan woman was a radical no-no in those days. But for Him to ask to drink from the same water jar her lips drank from was an "Oh no, He didn't!" moment for sure.

Jesus had a habit of breaking the traditional rules of the day to show His Father's love. Healing on the Sabbath? *Why not?* Sharing a meal with a thieving tax collector? *Let's do it!* Charging into the Temple with a whip and cleaning house? *You bet!*

I love this man!!

I feel a bit uncomfortable saying that Jesus had a habit of breaking the rules, but I don't feel uncomfortable in the least saying that

Jesus had a habit of breaking down walls. The wall in this passage was tall, thick, and strong; but Jesus was up to the challenge.

THE RACIST ROUTE

This story starts off with one of the only statements in Scripture I have ever questioned: "He (Jesus) had to go through Samaria." I question it because Jesus really didn't *have* to go through Samaria. He could have bypassed it. The region of Samaria lay between the Jewish territories of Judea, to the south, and Galilee, to the north. While making their way from Judea to Galilee, or vice-versa, the Jews in Jesus' time would typically avoid Samaria by crossing the Jordan River and traveling on the east side. Then after they had gone far enough, they would cross the Jordan again and enter either Galilee or Judea.

Why would the Jews go to such great lengths to skirt around Samaria, especially since this diversionary route cost them a lot of extra miles? And I'm not talking about traveling those miles in a brand-new Escalade with 22-inch wheels, TV monitors throughout, Bose sound system, and cool AC pumping through the vents. I'm talking about walking every step of the way in the heat of the Middle East. Folks, that's some serious hatred—or in this case, some serious racism.

About seven hundred years before Jesus was born, God allowed the people of the northern kingdom of Israel to be conquered by Assyria because of their sinful rebellion and blatant disloyalty to Him. Many thousands of Israelites were taken into exile in Assyria, and the Assyrians brought Gentiles into the land to take their place. The intermarriage of those Gentiles with the Israelites who were left behind resulted in the mixed race known as the Samaritans.

John 4:9 tells us that the woman was surprised by Jesus' re-quest for a drink because Jews refused to have anything to do with Samaritans. A Jew would be deemed ceremonially, or spiritually, unclean if he used a drinking container touched by a Samaritan, since the Jews considered all Samaritans "unclean." I believe the Jews' bigotry toward the Samaritans was the reason Jesus "had to go through" Samaria. There were other travel alternatives, for sure—but not for the man who came to break down walls.

ONE STEP FORWARD, TWO STEPS BACK

We have come a long way toward racial equality in today's world because of individuals who decided to confront walls of racism. Individuals like Abraham Lincoln, the sixteenth president of the United States, who on January 1, 1863 issued the Emancipation Proclamation, which forever freed all slaves in the Confederacy. And individuals like Martin Luther King Jr., whose "I Have a Dream" speech, given on August 28, 1963 on the steps of the Lincoln Memorial in front of 250,000 civil rights supporters, called for an end to racism in the United States.

King began that speech, which was ranked the top American speech of the twentieth century by a poll of scholars of public ad-dress in 1999, with these words:

> I am happy to join with you today in what will go down in history as the greatest demonstration for freedom in the history of our nation. Five score years ago, a great American, in whose symbolic shadow we stand today, signed the Emancipation Proclamation. This momentous decree came as a great beacon light of hope to millions of Negro slaves who had been

seared in the flames of withering injustice. It came
as a joyous daybreak to end the long night of their
captivity. But one hundred years later, the Negro still
is not free.

King's point was valid; one hundred years had passed since
Lincoln ordered the Emancipation Proclamation, yet much re-
mained unchanged. Two thousand years have passed in the history
of the church, and much remains unchanged for us as well. We are
still as segregated today as we were when the Jews were walking
many miles out of their way to avoid Samaria.

As a nation of manifold races and ethnicities, we live in com-
munities together, work together, go to school together, compete
in athletics together. But our worship on Sunday morning is where
it stops. We build our walls tall and thick and portray a beautiful picture of unity by putting a cross on the roof. The church in
America, however, is anything but united.

GOD'S HEART

Yet the Scriptures reveal God's heart for a completely different church.

> "I am praying not only for these disciples but also for
> all who will ever believe in me through their message.
> *I pray that they will all be one, just as you and I are
> one*—as you are in me, Father, and I am in you. . . .
> *May they experience such perfect unity that the world
> will know that you sent me and that you love them as
> much as you love me.*" – John 17:20–23

For Christ Himself has brought peace to us. He united Jews and Gentiles into one people when, in his own body on the cross, *he broke down the wall of hostility that separated us.* He did this by ending the system of law with its commandments and regulations. *He made peace between Jews and Gentiles by creating in himself one new people from the two groups.* Together as one body, Christ reconciled both groups to God by means of his death on the cross, and our hostility toward each other was put to death. – Ephesians 2:14–16

Always be humble and gentle. Be patient with each other, making allowance for each other's faults because of your love. *Make every effort to keep yourselves united in the Spirit, binding yourselves together with peace. For there is one body and one Spirit, just as you have been called to one glorious hope for the future.* – Ephesians 4:2–4

And they sang a new song with these words: "You are worthy to take the scroll and break its seal and open it. For you were slaughtered, and *your blood has ransomed people for God from every tribe and language and people and nation.* And you have called them to become a Kingdom of priests for our God." – Revelation 5:9–10

After this I saw a vast crowd, too great to count, from every nation and tribe and people and language, standing in front of the throne and before the Lamb. They were clothed in white robes and held palm branches in their hands. And they were shouting with a great roar, "Salvation comes from our God who sits on the throne and from the Lamb!" – Revelation 7:9–10

Why do the Scriptures speak so strongly against racism? Why would Jesus pass through Samaria and have a conversation with a promiscuous Samaritan woman by a well? For the same reasons, I believe, that Abraham Lincoln and Martin Luther King Jr. fought so hard to bring down the wall of racism in their day—because when walls fall down, people are truly set free.

A Wall Close to Home

My mother is a beautiful woman with an amazing heart, a desire to serve others above herself. My dad spent many nights on the road because of his work, but my mom always came through for me. Though she worked two jobs so I would always have everything I needed, she spent quality time with me as well. She would throw a baseball with me in the front yard or run football plays with me and my friends in the backyard. And she was quite the daredevil too, as a photograph in my office reveals: Mom is riding on the back of a motorcycle with me when I was only seven years old!

I have an amazing mom. But like many of us, my mother had a wall that needed to be confronted. And her test came in the year 2000 with the birth of a child.

After I played baseball overseas, my wife and I came back home eager to start a family. After many months with no success, followed by many tests, the doctor came to the conclusion that Amy had endometriosis and would need to have surgery. I can still hear the first words Amy spoke when she woke up in the recovery room: "Can we have children now?" It broke my heart that my wife's greatest desire was to be a mother but we were having no success.

After surgery we tried to conceive for several more years but eventually became convinced that we would never have a child. I watched Amy slowly slip into a state of depression. It didn't help that everyone at our church was getting pregnant. Amy began to cry out and seriously question God. One day I tried to cheer her up by flexing my muscles and saying, "Baby, look at me—aren't I enough?" She looked at me and screamed, "No, you're not!"

I would have felt really bad had I not remembered Elkanah, Hannah's husband, who made this comment while trying to console her when she couldn't have a child: "Why be downhearted just because you have no children? You have me—isn't that better than having ten sons?" (1 Samuel 1:8). I learned in that moment to trust God and to be patient with my wife and our circumstances.

And then, after many nights of praying, Amy and I decided that God was calling us to adopt a child. I was very excited to be moving toward fatherhood at last, and equally excited that Amy would finally have a chance to be the mother she desired to be.

Much of that excitement disappeared, however, when Amy told me she felt called to adopt a biracial child. What would people think? Would they assume Amy had been previously married, or that she had an affair and I decided to stay with her anyway? Would people whisper behind closed doors? And how would people respond to us in public? Would our church, which was predominantly white, fully accept us and our child?

All these questions raged in my heart, but through many hours of praying I realized this was God's call for our lives—and I decided to walk through that door boldly and proudly. After all, if the entire world rejected us, we would still have each other.

So Amy and I signed up at a local adoption agency and went through the rigorous process of adopting a biracial baby. We paid the adoption agency and the lawyer, went to the doctor for our physicals, and had the home studies. We did everything we needed to do, but one thing that we really couldn't have prepared for was the opposition of my mother and her side of the family. When I called to tell her about our decision to adopt a biracial child, her reaction was negative to say the least.

STRONG WORDS

A few days later, Mom called and invited me to lunch in downtown Charlotte. I knew I was up for the battle of a lifetime, because my mom's job was arguing in court on behalf of companies who were being sued by employees injured on the job. She had a reputation for putting up a good fight and saving corporations a lot of money.

Nevertheless, I felt prepared as I walked into the restaurant—until I saw that my mom's sister was joining us for lunch. It had been a while since I had seen my aunt, due to the fact that she rarely made an appearance at any family gathering other than Christmas and perhaps Easter. I suddenly felt like I was in one of those 1980s WWF cage matches and my mom had a partner to tag when she was ready to come out of the ring.

I sat down to share a meal and some conversation and waited for the match to begin. Little did I know that my aunt would go straight for the three-count by coming off the ropes with a fly-ing-scissor death-move, demanding, "Why would you adopt a black baby? Why would you hurt your mother and this family that way? No one in the family is going to accept a black baby."

My aunt had made this comment to a guy who has Exodus 15:3—"The Lord is a man of war, the Lord is His name"—tat-tooed on his right shoulder. She had to know that I would fight back. And grace wasn't what I was feeling at that moment. The first thing that popped into my head wasn't the fruit of the Spirit listed in Galatians 5:22—love, joy, peace, patience, kindness, goodness, faithfulness, gentleness, and self-control.

After pausing for a moment, I calmly tried to convey to my aunt that since I see her only once a year, at Christmas, her opinion was neither respected nor valid in my life. Then I looked at my mother and told her that she had a wall of racism in her heart and it needed to be confronted. I shared that it was hard for me to believe she could be in love with Christ and have such an attitude of hatred toward any child created by God. I pointed out to her verses like 1 John 5:1: "Everyone who believes that Jesus is the Christ has become a child of God. And everyone who loves the Father loves his children, too."

Mom glared at me with a stern look and informed me that she wasn't a racist and that she knew her Bible very well and went to church every Sunday. She went on to tell me she was extremely disappointed that I would do this and that things would probably never be the same.

I came home from that meeting extremely wounded, but I still believed God could do a work in Mom's heart. Every night, Amy and I prayed for the child God wanted us to welcome into our family. And we prayed that my mom and my family would confront the wall of racism that existed in their lives. We didn't have any more discussions with Mom about our plans, so we hoped and prayed that she would be ready to accept and support our next steps.

MALACHI ARRIVES!

Finally the day came when our son, Malachi Christian Marcellus Chapman, was born. We gave him the name Malachi after the

Old Testament prophet; and Christian as a follower of Christ; and Marcellus after his biological father, who—along with Malachi's biological mother—made the godly choice not to abort but to give life; and the name Chapman because that just comes with the deal, baby!

I will never forget the first time I saw my son. He was the most beautiful thing my eyes had ever seen: seven and a half pounds; twenty-one inches long; beautiful brown skin, brown eyes, and curly brown hair. Everything happened so fast that we hadn't even had a chance to call our parents and inform them that they were grandparents. Finally I was able to get ahold of my mom, and I screamed out, "Mom, you're a nana!"

My mom got extremely excited and immediately asked if we had adopted a little white child. I said, "No, Mom, we didn't."

She then asked if we adopted a child from China. I answered, "No, Mom, we didn't."

Then she asked if the child was Latino, to which I replied, "Nope."

Then, after a long pause, she asked if we adopted a biracial child. With great enthusiasm, I responded, "Yes we did, Mom—and he's beautiful!"

I wasn't prepared for the words I heard in return. "Well, I'm sorry to hear that." And then she hung up.

My mom's reaction broke my heart and crushed my spirit, but beyond that it confused me. My mother was raised in church and confessed to be a follower of Christ. We went to church every Sunday morning, read our Bibles faithfully, and said our prayers at every meal. Mom supported me when I got baptized at age twelve, came to hear me sing musicals at church, and kept me plugged into Wednesday night youth meetings and summer camp. How could this woman of God whom I loved and respected have such a wall of racism in her heart?

THE WALL CRUMBLES

Three weeks went by without any contact at all between Mom and me. Then one day I heard a knock at our front door. I was shocked to open the door and see my mom standing there. Though she had a look of frustration and anger on her face, she asked if she could come in and see our son. When I left the room to ask Amy to bring Malachi out to see his nana, she informed me that I better be on the lookout and guard him with my life!

Because Mom's decisions had broken a lot of trust, her walls had affected Amy and me as well. I won't get into that any further, other than to say that we always need to remember that walls not only affect us but others too—which is one more reason why it's so important to confront them and tear them down.

After I assured Amy that everything would be OK, Mom came and sat down in the rocking chair we had just bought to rock Malachi to sleep while feeding him at night. Amy brought Malachi into the room wearing his New York Yankees onesie. I know I'm a proud father, but I'm telling you, he was as beautiful as any child you've ever laid eyes on. I took Malachi gently into my arms and laid him in Mom's lap. Amy and I then sat back and watched for several minutes to see how she would respond.

Mom just sat there at first, but after about five minutes she began to rock Malachi slowly back and forth in the chair. At the ten-minute mark we saw the first tear fall from Mom's eyes and land on Malachi's chest. And at the fifteen-minute mark my mother was crying uncontrollably while holding the grandson she had just met.

I looked at Amy—who, like me, had tears in her eyes—and told her that Mom just gave her life to Jesus Christ. You see, in that moment a wall came down in my mother's life. You could almost feel the Spirit of God in the room and hear the angels sing as she experienced being free for the first time in her life. Even though I've never been a fan of WWF wrestling, I realized I had a tag-team partner that day, and His name was Jesus. For six months I had wrestled with my mom and her wall, but that day I tagged my partner and before long He broke down her wall, and it was a quick "1, 2, 3—you're out!"

Today my mother is the most wonderful grandmother any three grandchildren could have. In fact, our boys would rather be with Nana than with me and Amy! And the demolition of Mom's wall had a great impact in helping her sister's wall to fall. Aunt Linda has become a huge part of our children's lives, and she loves them like her own grandchildren. This is yet another example of how our walls, and their destruction, impact others—either negatively or positively.

DOWN FOR THE COUNT

How long had Mom lived behind her wall? How many relationships had been severed because others couldn't get past it?

Those questions are begging this one as well: How many years have you held on to your wall? How many relationships have been severed and destroyed because you are still trapped behind a wall that needs to come down? Only you can answer that.

For the woman at the well, enough was enough. She realized after Jesus confronted her that her wall needed to come down. My favorite part of her story is told in John 4:27–29:

> Just then his disciples came back. They were shocked to find him talking to a woman, but none of them had the nerve to ask, "What do you want with her?" or "Why are you talking to her?" The woman left

her water jar beside the well and ran back to the village, telling everyone, "Come and see a man who told me everything I ever did! Could he possibly be the Messiah?"

Why would the disciples lack the nerve to ask Jesus those questions? I believe the answer can be found in John 2:13–17:

> It was nearly time for the Jewish Passover celebration, so Jesus went to Jerusalem. In the Temple area he saw merchants selling cattle, sheep, and doves for sacrifices; he also saw dealers at tables exchanging foreign money. Jesus made a whip from some ropes and chased them all out of the Temple. He drove out the sheep and cattle, scattered the money changers' coins over the floor, and turned over their tables. Then, going over to the people who sold doves, he told them, "Get these things out of here. Stop turning my Father's house into a marketplace!" Then his disciples remembered this prophecy from the Scriptures: "Passion for God's house will consume me."

This passage has passion all over it. In fact, the disciples actually remembered the prophecy from Psalm 69: "Passion for God's house will consume me." To put it another way, Jesus is consumed with you. He is passionate to have a relationship with you. He is prepared to chase out the enemy and fight for your heart in order to seal your name in the Lamb's Book of Life.

How is this going to happen? There's only one way. Let the wall fall down. Let go of the wall you have been holding on to and let Jesus swing the sledge, or His whip, till it's gone.

My mom was raised in a home in which racism was a way of life. So the wall she finally confronted had been in existence for over fifty years. Jesus knew that the woman at the well had previously had five different husbands, and she wasn't even married to the man she was with at the time. So her wall had surely been erected for way too long as well.

How long will it take you to let go? How tightly are you holding on to what needs to be torn down? Only you and the Lord can take care of this. So I would encourage you to tag Him and let Him enter the ring. He's ready to spring off the top rope at any time. Can you hear that—"1, 2, …"?

The choice is yours.

UNITED WE STAND, DIVIDED WE FALL

All the believers devoted themselves
to the apostles' teaching, and to
fellowship, and to sharing in meals
(including the Lord's Supper),
and to prayer.
A deep sense of awe came
over them all, and the apostles
performed many miraculous signs
and wonders. And all the believers
met together in one place and
shared everything they had.

– Acts 2:42–44

CHAPTER 11

A WALL OF DISUNITY

From 1998 to 2002 I had the privilege of serving as the college pastor at Downtown Community Fellowship in Clemson, South Carolina. My primary responsibilities were to speak at the three Sunday night services and to disciple young men who attended Clemson University. I led a weekly Bible study, met with guys one-on-one, and held open Q and A sessions in which students could just bring it and sling it.

But I have to admit that my favorite activity was our monthly guys' night out, where we could get together and just be guys. We put our baseball caps on backwards, ate hot wings with our elbows on the table, and got loud without any ladies next to us telling us we were embarrassing them. Usually we would go watch a guys' movie. I saw a lot of movies during my four years there, but none was better than *The Last Samurai.*

Now I'm not a big fan of Tom Cruise, and I certainly don't agree with him in regard to Scientology. But I had to admit that this movie was amazing from start to finish. Cruise plays the role of Captain Nathan Algren, a veteran of the Civil War and Indian Wars who is haunted by his memories of massacring Native Americans during the Indian Wars. Needing the income, he agrees to help the Japanese government teach men how to fight the American way—with rifles, Gatling guns, and cannons—in order to put down a samurai rebellion.

While Algren is training the Japanese soldiers, the samurai launch a sneak attack. Algren is taken captive and forced to live with the samurai in their village deep inside the mountains. There he falls in love with the samurai way of life and loyalty to their traditions. In one profound scene, we hear Algren's thoughts while he is watching the people: "I've never been a churchgoing man, and what I've seen on the field of battle has led me to question God's purpose. But there is indeed something spiritual in this place. And though it may forever be obscure to me, I cannot but be aware of its power. I do know that it is here that I've known my first untroubled sleep in many years."

By the end of the movie, Algren has joined the samurai clan. I remember thinking to myself, *This is how the Christian community is supposed to look. We should be so attractive, so powerful, so united in purpose, that people are drawn to us.*

Ask yourself if that is what the church in America looks like today. Are people so attracted to the flow of life in our churches that they line up to get in the doors every Sunday?

ALL TOGETHER

Let's look at a passage of Scripture that reveals who we are called to be as followers of Christ and as the church:

> All the believers devoted themselves to the apostles' teaching, and to fellowship, and to sharing in meals (including the Lord's Supper), and to prayer.
>
> A deep sense of awe came over them all, and the apostles performed many miraculous signs and wonders. And all the believers met together in one place and shared everything they had. They sold their property and possessions and shared the money with those in need. They worshiped together at the Temple each day, met in homes for the Lord's Supper, and shared their meals with great joy and generosity—all the while praising God and enjoying the goodwill of all the people. And each day the Lord added to their fellowship those who were being saved. – Acts 2:42–47

We could focus on many wonderful things in this passage: the generosity of the early church to sell what they had to give to those in need; the signs and wonders which confirmed that the Holy Spirit was at work and drew thousands of people to see what God would do next; the fact that the believers met to worship God in the Temple every day, which smacks all those today who complain about going to church one day a week. What inspires me the most, however, is the unity that is so evident. The very first word in the passage—*all*—reveals a lot about the early church. Luke, the author of Acts, used that word several times here. And another word that is used more than once in the passage is *together*.

These two words demonstrate the character and vitality of the church in the first days of Christianity, which revolved around the unity they shared as believers. There were no Episcopalians, Presbyterians, Catholics, Lutherans, Methodists, Baptists, or Assemblies of God. (If I didn't mention your denomination, please don't take offense. There are way too many to list—which is really the point I'm trying to make.) In the early church there was only one body of believers, and they did everything together to make an impact for the kingdom of God.

The early church could draw a crowd, and that crowd experienced signs and wonders, teaching, and fellowship at such an amazing level that each and every day people gave their lives to Christ. Today in the United States we have so much separation, so much arguing over doctrine, such a lack of unity, that very few are being drawn to the message of Christ. Surveys have shown a decrease in church involvement among Americans over the years.

However, there are reports that the gospel is exploding in many countries around the world today—forcing us to ask, "What's the difference?" I believe the church is growing in these places because Christians are united and have set aside their personal differences to come together to build God's kingdom through a relationship with Jesus Christ.

"THE CHURCH OF UGANDA"

Recently I was speaking at a Christian school and found myself trying to break through many walls and barriers to get the gospel into the teenagers' hearts. So I posted a tweet requesting prayer. Because I was discerning intense spiritual warfare, I appealed for prayer warriors to go to battle with me. I received many comments, but none as powerful as an e-mail from a pastor in Uganda.

He said he had gotten my request and that the church of Uganda would be fasting and praying for me that week. I wrote back asked him what he meant by "the church of Uganda," and he replied that at least seventy-five churches were already fasting and praying for me and others would be joining as they heard the request.

I couldn't believe it. But I could sense the effect of this unity: I felt the Spirit of God as I preached, and I saw the work of His hands on the hearts of those who were lost and hurting. By the end of the week, almost two hundred kids made decisions for Christ. And let me assure you, this was no small feat. To have a breakthrough at a Christian school can be a huge miracle, since you're dealing with kids who feel they have heard it all before and have everything they need. I knew that unless the Holy Spirit showed up, very few walls would crumble while I was there.

I'm convinced that the breakthrough came for one reason: "The church of Uganda" had pulled together and taken my request before the Lord.

I'm reminded of when the Holy Spirit poured Himself out on the disciples at Pentecost. Let's take a look at that passage and consider what brought about this visitation, because I don't think anyone reading this would disagree that we need more fellowship with the Spirit in our churches today.

> On the day of Pentecost all the believers were meeting together in one place. Suddenly, there was a sound from heaven like the roaring of a mighty windstorm, and it filled the house where they were sitting. Then, what looked like flames or tongues of fire appeared and settled on each of them. – Acts 2:1–3

Did you notice the invitation that was extended to the Holy Spirit? "*All* the believers were meeting *together* in one place." The key to success was the disciples being in unity and ready to work together to extend the gospel and build God's kingdom. I believe this is how we will see revival come to our country and our churches. In fact, every time I speak at an event and see that churches are working together in the community I know God is going to do great things—because this is our blueprint for spiritual success.

Painful Lessons

There was a time in my life when I didn't understand the importance of unity within the entire body of Christ. My plan was to graduate from college and then become a pastor in the denomination in which I grew up. But as God would have it, He introduced me to a man named John Reeves who discipled me during my college days in regard to the true meaning of church and of being a follower of Christ. John was the pastor of Downtown Community Fellowship, a church plant that initially met in a bar across the street from Clemson University. Before long this group of 50 people grew to about 750, and I was fortunate to become one of the teaching pastors and watch this growth take place.

I became very unpopular on the campus of my denomination's college, where I was majoring in religion, because I was involved in a church that wasn't part of that denomination and tradition. Some of the other religion majors would visit DCF just to listen to me preach so they could try to catch me in a doctrinal trap. This was very frustrating for me, but all the while John Reeves continued to mentor me. And the more time I spent with John, the more questions I had for my professors.

One of my professors tried to explain the value of denominations by sharing an illustration with me. He compared denominations to many sailboats on the ocean. Built and crafted differently, the sailboats come in different shapes and sizes and have different-colored sails. But they are all sailing in the same direction. He said the Holy Spirit is the wind that blows those sails and takes them all on the same route, which leads to God. The denominations might all look different, but they are all heading in the same direction.

I had to admit this was a beautiful way of viewing denominations, and I knew the professor's heart was pure in regard to Jesus and the church. But I still saw one problem with his illustration. Although the Holy Spirit blows into the sails and tries to guide the denominations in the way they should go, each sailboat has a rudder and therefore the option to turn and go its own way. My response was that it would be a beautiful thing if the professor's illustration was being fulfilled, but in my opinion a lot of boats are lost at sea—driven by their own desire to steer the church in the way they feel it should go.

For instance, we have mainline Protestant churches that have walked away from the authority of God's Word when it comes to homosexuality and other foundational biblical teachings. We have churches that feel their Calvinistic approach to biblical interpretation is right and everyone else is wrong, while other churches feel that their Arminian perspective is the only way. We have Baptist churches that think their approach to evangelism is really the only means to get the gospel to a lost world. We have Pentecostal churches that think other Christians aren't actually saved because they don't speak in tongues or operate in the gifts of the Spirit like they do. And we have nondenominational churches that think no one else measures up to their cutting-edge style of worship.

Meanwhile, we forget there is great power in unity and in the message of love being extended through the spirit of togetherness that God has desired for His people all along. I love the church, and my desire is not to scold people but to encourage us to come together—because we are stronger when we combine our numbers in full force.

In Charlotte, North Carolina, where I live, we have over seven hundred churches. I have often wondered what it would look like if all the churches came together on a Sunday and held a service in the football stadium downtown where the Carolina Panthers play. Can you imagine what it would be like if more than fifty thousand people worshiped the Lord together? Can you imagine the press it would get, and how it would inspire churches around the world to come together? Can you imagine what the Spirit of the Lord would do with that kind of unity? In my humble opinion, it's worth trying.

DENOMINATIONAL DIVERSIONS

One day I got a call from a young man who had worshiped at Downtown Community Fellowship in Clemson before becoming the youth pastor at a Methodist Church. He had worked hard to convince the church leaders that in order to reach the lost, especially younger people, they needed more than just a traditional service. They agreed to begin a new contemporary worship service, and the young associate wanted me to come and speak at their launch.

I gladly accepted the invitation, but things started to get weird as the date of the event got closer. The senior pastor asked questions about my denominational background and about whether I had Methodist training. Then he requested that I submit my sermon for his approval. It seemed like he was squeezing the new youth pastor every way he could in order to squash this new approach to evangelism.

The day finally came for me to speak, and as I drove toward the church I was blown away by the opportunity this congregation has to reach the lost. The church is located in a resort town right next to the water's edge, where thousands back their boats into the water's edge and lounge in the sun while listening to the sounds of a live band playing at the nearest bar. And boy do they have bars to choose from! Within a quarter of a mile of the church are no less than ten bars—filled every Friday and Saturday night with people looking for answers. I was thrilled that this new service was going to reach out with those answers.

When I arrived at the church I could feel the excitement of the people as the service was about to begin. The coffee was great, the smiles were genuine, the platform was creative, and the worship was spot on. When I stepped up to preach, nearly five hundred people—an awesome crowd for a first service—were ready to hear a word from the Lord. I had a wonderful time encouraging them to be the church, and then we enjoyed some good food and fellowship afterward. I can still see the excited look on the youth pastor's face in light of what God had done and how the people had rallied around the vision.

A week later that satisfied smile turned to a frustrated frown. The youth pastor called to tell me the senior pastor informed him that only Methodist-trained preachers would be allowed to speak at future services and that he personally would be speaking at the next one. Even though the senior pastor wasn't gifted at communicating the gospel to a crowd of lost young people, he felt the need to take control and do things according to the traditions of the Methodist Church.

I wonder if he thinks those who are lost really care about the Methodist way. Does he think they would rather hear about John Wesley, the founder of Methodism, or about Jesus, who gave His life for the sins of the world?

Don't get me wrong—I love John Wesley! This man played a huge role in bringing revival to two different continents. He was known for his radical preaching and passionate approach to getting out the message of Jesus to the lost. John's brother Charles, his worship leader, had a radical approach to ministry as well. He would take the tunes played in bars and put Christian words to them, and then sing those songs in their meetings. If that's not edgy, I don't know what is!

It's All about Jesus

That being said, at the end of the day it's about Jesus, not about our denominational preferences. What potential this church's contemporary service would have had if this traditional pastor would have gotten out of the way and let it be about Jesus. I believe this service could be packed with people and testimonies of salvation. But instead they barely meet once a month and are no more going after the lost than are the owners of the bars next door. I know this sounds harsh, but I believe we need to start calling it like we see it.

The Christian group 4Him had many hits in the 90s, but none was more popular than "The Basics of Life." This song calls us to get back to the basics of life—essentially faith, hope, and love. I completely agree, and I think the basics of the Christian community can be found in the unity and togetherness we see displayed in Acts 2:42–47. Though I love the church, I believe denominationalism has caused a huge divide in this country. We need to remember what Jesus said in Matthew 12:25: "Any kingdom divided by civil war is doomed. A town or family splintered by feuding will fall apart."

If we don't begin to come together, we are doomed. My desire is for the church to grow and be all that God calls it to be. I see so much potential and so much zeal and passion for growth; yet too often leadership controls and contains this passion because of a greater love for denomination than for unity. Our God is too powerful, the message of Christ and forgiveness is too needed, and the Holy Spirit is too readily available to keep this wall of separation up any longer.

I am just now starting a new venture in ministry in response to a call God has placed on my heart to plant a church. We have chosen the name "Radiant Church," which comes from Psalm 34:5: "Those who look to him for help will be radiant with joy; no shadow of shame will darken their faces." Our team, represented by several cultures and races, is very diverse.

Our goal is to make sure everything we do is driven by God's Word, especially the book of Acts, which we feel is the perfect outline for success. We have decided not to have formal membership. Instead, after people get saved and baptized we will disciple them to understand they are a part of the broader church—the body of Christ—not just Radiant Church. We'll make an effort to join together as much as possible with nearby churches for cookouts, service projects, and even joint worship services where fellow pastors and worship leaders will take the stage together as one for the kingdom.

We believe that if we join together as the early church did in Acts 2:42–47, we will enjoy the growth and spiritual success that God has promised when His people come together. We hope this small effort on our part will spark other local churches to do the same, eventually spreading around the world before it's all said and done.

What part will you play? Remember that in the first part of Acts 2 the Spirit came at Pentecost because the disciples were together in one place. Remember the words of Jesus in John 17:20–21: "I am praying not only for these disciples but also for all who will ever believe in me through their message. I pray that they will all be *one*, just as you and I are *one*—as you are in me, Father, and I am in you. And may they be in us so that the world will believe you sent me."

Come on folks, we can't come together if a wall stands between us. Let's tear down that wall and start to live out our unity as the body of Christ. If we can't worship together here on earth, what makes us think we can go to heaven and worship together there for eternity? If we can't get it right here, I don't think God will allow us the chance to mess up His plan. He is building a home of unity for *all* people to come *together* as *one* and worship forever. Now that's worth tearing down a wall to experience, don't you think?

Got Blood On Ya?

And if you do not carry your
own cross and follow me, you
cannot be my disciple.

– Luke 14:27

CHAPTER 12

A WALL OF HYPOCRISY

Like me, you've probably heard about surveys reporting that the most common reason people give for not going to church is because they feel the church is full of hypocrites. When people identify themselves to me as Christians, I often ask them, "Got blood on ya?" Most folks are confused by that question, but it opens the door for me to provide an explanation. Jesus said, "If you do not carry your own cross and follow me, you cannot be my disciple" (Luke 14:27). You can't call yourself a follower of Christ if you don't sacrifice for Him—and get some blood on ya.

THE FIRST MARTYR

Now before you tune me out and say, "I know I'm a Christian— so, yeah, I must have some blood on me," let me share with you a passage in the book of Acts that reinforces why it's so important that we live out Luke 14:27. As we look at the story of Stephen, the first martyr of the church, we see a great example of a man who got some blood on him. Stephen preached a passionate, in-your-face message to his fellow Jews who had rejected Jesus as Messiah. Let's see what happened next.

> The Jewish leaders were infuriated by Stephen's accusation, and they shook their fists at him in rage. But Stephen, full of the Holy Spirit, gazed steadily into heaven and saw the glory of God, and he saw Jesus standing in the place of honor at God's right hand. And he told them, "Look, I see the heavens opened and the Son of Man standing in the place of honor at God's right hand!" – Acts 7:54–56

If the Jewish leaders had been infuriated by Stephen's sermon, they got *really* infuriated when he said he saw the heavens opened and the Son of Man standing in the place of honor at God's right hand. Just a few years earlier Jesus had stood before these same Jewish leaders, who asked Him if He was Israel's Messiah. Jesus answered, "I Am. And you will see the Son of Man seated in the place of power at God's right hand and coming on the clouds of heaven" (Mark 14:62).

Because of His answer, Jesus was pronounced guilty of blasphemy and condemned to death. Unless the Jewish leaders were ready to repent and admit their terrible error of rejecting Jesus, they had no option but to find Stephen guilty of blasphemy too. That is exactly what they did, as we can tell from their actions.

> Then they put their hands over their ears and began shouting. They rushed at him and dragged him out of

the city and began to stone him. His accusers took off
their coats and laid them at the feet of a young man
named Saul.

As they stoned him, Stephen prayed, "Lord Jesus,
receive my spirit." He fell to his knees, shouting,
"Lord, don't charge them with this sin!" And with
that, he died. – Acts 7:57–60

After reading about Stephen's fate, let me encourage you to
stop and ask yourself if you would have been willing to sign up to
be a disciple in those days.

Nevertheless, let's see what happened to the church because
this man followed Christ, carried his own cross, and therefore got
some blood on him.

A great wave of persecution began that day, sweeping
over the church in Jerusalem; and all the believers except the apostles were scattered through the regions of
Judea and Samaria. (Some devout men came and bur-
ied Stephen with great mourning.) But Saul was going everywhere to destroy the church. He went from
house to house, dragging out both men and women
to throw them into prison.

But the believers who were scattered preached
the Good News about Jesus wherever they went.
– Acts 8:1–4

Take a look at the last verse again. According to this passage, as well as others throughout the book of Acts, the gospel
was proclaimed and spread because of the persecution that took
place. Since believers were willing to get blood on them—taking
up their cross and carrying it boldly, even unto death—the church

was growing unlike anything we have seen since that time. And I believe we will experience revival when Christians begin living out the book of Acts again by being in unity and making sacrifices on behalf of the kingdom of God. Talk about crashing down a wall of hypocrisy!

TAKING UP YOUR CROSS

Before you sign up to carry your own cross, I think it's important to present the context associated with Jesus taking up His cross. Let's pick up the story after Jesus affirmed to the Jewish leaders that He was the Messiah.

> Then the high priest tore his clothing to show his horror and said, "Why do we need other witnesses? You have all heard his blasphemy. What is your verdict?"
>
> "Guilty!" they all cried. "He deserves to die!"
>
> Then some of them began to spit at him, and they blindfolded him and beat him with their fists. "Prophesy to us," they jeered. And the guards slapped him as they took him away. . . .
>
> Very early in the morning the leading priests, the elders, and the teachers of religious law—the entire high council—met to discuss their next step. They bound Jesus, led him away, and took him to Pilate, the Roman governor. . . .
>
> Now it was the governor's custom each year during the Passover celebration to release one prisoner—anyone the people requested. One of the prisoners at that time was Barabbas, a revolutionary who had committed murder in an uprising. The crowd

went to Pilate and asked him to release a prisoner as usual.

"Would you like me to release to you this 'King of the Jews'?" Pilate asked. (For he realized by now that the leading priests had arrested Jesus out of envy.) But at this point the leading priests stirred up the crowd to demand the release of Barabbas instead of Jesus. Pilate asked them, "Then what should I do with this man you call the king of the Jews?"

They shouted back, "Crucify him!"

"Why?" Pilate demanded. "What crime has he committed?"

But the mob roared even louder, "Crucify him!"

So to pacify the crowd, Pilate released Barabbas to them. He ordered Jesus flogged with a lead-tipped whip, then turned him over to the Roman soldiers to be crucified.

The soldiers took Jesus into the courtyard of the governor's headquarters (called the Praetorium) and called out the entire regiment. They dressed him in a purple robe, and they wove thorn branches into a crown and put it on his head. Then they saluted him and taunted, "Hail! King of the Jews!" And they struck him on the head with a reed stick, spit on him, and dropped to their knees in mock worship. When they were finally tired of mocking him, they took off the purple robe and put his own clothes on him again. Then they led him away to be crucified.

A passerby named Simon, who was from Cyrene, was coming in from the countryside just then, and the soldiers forced him to carry Jesus' cross. (Simon was the father of Alexander and Rufus.) And they brought

Jesus to a place called Golgotha (which means "Place of the Skull"). They offered him wine drugged with myrrh, but he refused it.

Then the soldiers nailed him to the cross. They divided his clothes and threw dice to decide who would get each piece. It was nine o'clock in the morning when they crucified him. A sign announced the charge against him. It read, "The King of the Jews." Two revolutionaries were crucified with him, one on his right and one on his left.

The people passing by shouted abuse, shaking their heads in mockery. "Ha! Look at you now!" they yelled at him. "You said you were going to destroy the Temple and rebuild it in three days. Well then, save yourself and come down from the cross!"

The leading priests and teachers of religious law also mocked Jesus. "He saved others," they scoffed, "but he can't save himself! Let this Messiah, this King of Israel, come down from the cross so we can see it and believe him!" Even the men who were crucified with Jesus ridiculed him. – Mark 14:63–65; 15:1,6–32

Does your practice of carrying your own cross look anything like this? Now you might be thinking, *Why does this guy want me to suffer like that?* I don't want you to suffer, nor do I want to myself. But the truth is that the kingdom grows through our sacrifice and blood—and it always has, according to the Word of God. This is proven through the growth happening in the churches around the world that are receiving the most persecution.

The "good news" is that our time, in my opinion, is coming very soon. Our country has taken prayer out of its schools and the Ten Commandments out of its courthouses. Many of our citizens, including our political leaders, claim to be Christians yet support things like gay marriage and late-term abortions. Our rebellion toward God and His Word is setting us up, I believe, on a course of great suffering and sacrifice. We are about to be given the opportunity to carry our cross through our blood, sweat, and tears. We are about to be *forced* to tear down our walls of hypocrisy.

Why is this "good news"? Once again, remember all the growth recorded in the book of Acts when the early Christians carried their cross and were persecuted. Suffering breeds growth!

AN AMAZING ASSEMBLY

Let me share with you a personal story along this line. As a traveling speaker, many of my ministry opportunities involve Christian schools, colleges, or youth conferences. Occasionally I receive an invitation to speak in a public school because of some aspect of my past: i.e., playing baseball in college and overseas, participating in a reality racing show on Spike TV, or experiencing the lure of drugs and the effects of addiction. But I had never been asked to speak on my faith and given an opportunity to share my testimony about Christ in a public school. So I was more than shocked when I was given the chance to do that in an assembly at the New Heights Middle School in Jefferson, South Carolina.

I knew that some local churches were going together to sponsor the assembly and that a Christian rapper would be there, but I just assumed that I would do the norm—speak about some facet of my past and weave in Christian values without mentioning Christianity per se. When I pulled into the school parking lot, the principal, Larry Stinson, met me outside. After introducing himself, Mr. Stinson told me, with an intense look on his face, that he was about to retire and had heard from God.

"Oh no!" I responded. Anytime God starts to speak in radical ways you can bet some blood is going to hit the floor, although the kingdom will grow by leaps and bounds. I got both excited and nervous as Mr. Stinson shared with me that six hundred middle school students would be in the gym and he wanted them to hear the gospel and have an opportunity to respond to an altar call. He informed me that he had arranged for a Christian rapper named B-SHOC to provide some Christian music and for adults from various churches to be ready to talk and pray with the students afterward.

I asked this man who was going all out for Jesus why he would risk everything for one shot at the kids' hearts. I can still see the passion on Mr. Stinson's face as he shared with me how he had walked the halls of the school every day for years, carrying a burning desire for the students to hear the truth before he retired. He said he would even like me to debunk evolution, and asked me how much time that would take. "About a minute and a half," I replied, "because science can't win against unconditional love."

Stating that he was tired of being a hypocrite, Mr. Stinson said he wanted to make sure the kids saw him living out his faith so they could have a chance to receive the love of Jesus. "In the end," he concluded, "that's the only thing that will matter."

I was blown away! Although I knew the persecution would be devastating—and I shared that perception with Mr. Stinson—I also knew that the impending growth of the kingdom would be worth the sacrifice.

B-SHOC had already taken the stage when I walked into the gymnasium. The excitement of the crowd was incredible—the kids were waving their arms from side to side and jumping up and down. When the concert ended, the students were asked to clear the gym floor and take a seat. As I was introduced, I was pumped about the battle I knew was about to take place.

There I was, face to face with six hundred middle school students and their teachers. I started off by discrediting evolution, which caused several teachers to squirm in their seats, and then I moved right to my testimony and a proclamation of the gospel based on John 4. Things got off to a slow start, I sensed, because the students were in shock that they were hearing something like this in their public school. But after a while they started to engage the message.

The kids were definitely tracking with me as I talked about Jesus breaking down walls of racism in order to love a Samaritan woman beside a well, as I talked about the sinless Son of God initiating a conversation with this woman who was sleeping with so many guys, as I talked about the fact that this woman—after encountering the source of living water and salvation—went back to the town to share her story with those who would have stoned her to death if they had known about her secrets. And their eyes filled with tears as I shared my story about how my parents' divorce led me into a life of alcohol, drugs, one-night stands, and spending time in jail. I affirmed that there is hope beyond what science can explain, relationships can provide, and wealth can buy.

I concluded by inviting those who wanted to confess their sins and receive Jesus, and His free but priceless gift of living water, to come down to the gym floor. Immediately a few kids headed for the floor, and soon students started flooding down. Before it was all said and done, 324 kids gave their lives to Jesus! They were taken to another room to be prayed for and given some information so that they could be discipled as they plugged into a local church.

The sponsoring churches had planned a follow-up meeting for the youth and their parents that evening at the school. So we got to share with some parents about what God had done that day, and around twenty parents came to Christ!

Enter the ACLU

All in all, one of my best days of ministry would soon turn into one of my greatest times of struggle. Someone had filmed B-SHOC performing and the students coming down to give their lives to Jesus and then posted it on YouTube, where the ACLU got a hold of it and charged that the school administrators had broken the law by violating the First Amendment's separation of church and state. Then the situation began making national news, which eventually led to *The New York Times* calling me and asking for an interview. I declined at first, but then changed my mind when they said they were going to write an article with or without my side of the story.

The wounds and insults started coming one after the other once the story made *The New York Times*. I received hate mail from all over the country and even attacks from members of the Christian community. For example, a woman in Michigan who had been a teacher for forty years wrote that she was disgusted with my actions, stating that presenting the gospel is meant for church on Sunday, not for schools and workplaces during the week. I responded by pointing out that Jesus said He didn't come to save the healthy but the sick, and then asked if she agreed with me that there are sick kids in schools and unhealthy coworkers in workplaces.

One of the most painful comments came from a teacher at the school where the assembly took place. I remembered her jumping up and down and cheering during the concert and crying tears of joy as the students made the decision to follow Jesus. But because the ACLU was trying to fire the principal and come down on the teachers, now she condemned B-SHOC and me for singing and preaching. And one of the churches in the area, which *The New York Times* contacted after they interviewed me, condemned the event, saying that the church should never take religion into the schools.

Let me tell you what this is all about. It's about church folks not wanting to be persecuted or face down the enemy. It's about the fear of losing their 501(c)(3) tax-exempt status. It's about being more concerned with what others think than what God thinks. It's about not wanting to get blood on ya. And at its core is a wall of hypocrisy.

PERSECUTION IS GOOD

Years ago I heard a story about a pastor in China who had been thrown into prison for preaching the gospel. The governing authorities told him that the only way he could be released and reunited with his wife and children was to recant the message of Jesus. After the pastor had been imprisoned for years, a Christian reporter from the United States was given the opportunity to interview him. Before ending their time together, the reporter asked the pastor if he had a prayer request to share with all the Christians in America who were lifting him up. The pastor looked at the reporter and said, "Tell them to pray for persecution. Persecution is good." He understood that persecution builds God's kingdom.

The persecution of the early Christians is why we are still talking about Jesus more than two thousand years later. Tertullian, a second-century church leader, wrote that "the blood of the martyrs is the seed of the church."

In addition to Stephen, the book of Acts recounts how James, the brother of John, became a martyr for the faith. Luke, the author of Acts, states in Acts 12:2 that James was "killed with a sword"—i.e., beheaded, like John the Baptist. Jesus told Peter, in John 21:18–19, that he would be martyred. Early and credible accounts reported that Peter was crucified upside down—as he requested because he didn't consider himself worthy to die the same way as his Lord Jesus—in Rome during Nero's reign.

There are traditional accounts, some more reliable than others, that all of Jesus' original apostles, with the exception of John, were martyred. The apostle Paul, though not one of the Twelve, wrote many of his letters to the churches he had founded throughout the Roman Empire while he was imprisoned because of his faith. And dependable early Christian tradition attests that Paul, like Peter, was martyred in Rome during Nero's reign, though by beheading rather than by crucifixion.

I would be doing the early Christians a great injustice if I didn't give them high praise for building a rock-solid foundation for the church. They used bone for brick and blood for mortar, and that foundation is still standing today. But I would be doing the church today a great injustice if I didn't warn that it has allowed an impeding wall to be built through the lack of sacrifice on the part of those who claim to be Christians. How can we get blood on us if we are hiding safely behind this wall? This wall could be standing because of fear, complacency, selfishness, pride, or just good old-fashioned laziness. Yet it can come down.

I didn't write this chapter to beat you up, but rather to challenge you to see the difference you can make if you will start to get a little blood on ya and go through a little persecution for the kingdom. According to Romans 5:3–5, persecution and trials not only build the church but enhance our personal lives as well.

> We can rejoice, too, when we run into problems and trials, for we know that they help us develop endurance. And endurance develops strength of character, and character strengthens our confident hope of salvation. And this hope will not lead to disappointment.

For we know how dearly God loves us, because he has
given us the Holy Spirit to fill our hearts with his love.

To finish the story about the assembly at the New Heights
Middle School, a Christian reporter told me during a phone interview that the court case between the ACLU and the school district
was settled out of court. As a result of these events, the superinten-
dent of the school district was reprimanded, the principal ended
up having to step down, and new rules have been set in place in
South Carolina that make it more difficult for anyone affiliated
with a religious group to share their beliefs.

I got a call from a friend of mine who is involved in state
politics in South Carolina, and he told me that the next "See You
at The Pole" day in South Carolina was the best attended in recent memory. The reason, he said, was because Christians in public
schools heard what happened with us and the ACLU and decided
they were going to stand strong.

During this trial we were all going through, I spoke with Mr.
Stinson and asked him how he was doing. He said he had never
been attacked like this in his life, noting that he had received hate
mail all the way from Switzerland. When I said, "Praise God for
that, Bro!" he responded, "I wish I could share your enthusiasm."

I tried to help this devout believer see the impact he was having because of the risk he had taken to extend the gospel to the
lost and because of the persecution he had experienced as a result.
"How many Christians can say that their Christianity made it half-
way around the world because of the radical stand and sacrifice
they were willing to make for the kingdom?" I asked him.

Mr. Stinson replied that he had never thought about his trials
and persecution like that. Have you?

Are you ready to see any and every wall in your life, including a subtle wall of hypocrisy, fall? Are you ready to get some blood on ya?

CONCLUSION

A WALL HAS FALLEN

I can do everything through Christ, who gives me
strength. – *Philippians 4:13*

JUSTIN "EFEOSA" WREN

I was about to speak at Kingdom Building Ministry's Deep Camp,
held every summer at the YMCA's picturesque Snow Mountain
Ranch in the Colorado mountains. I was standing in the back
during the worship time, watching people in order to get a feel
for where they were at spiritually. Some were clearly connecting
with the Lord, as they stood with their eyes closed and their hands
raised, while others appeared to be daydreaming or were talking to
the person next to them.

But then I noticed a young man who was hard to miss. He
was sporting a blonde mohawk and his 6'4", 265-pound frame was
sprawled out on the floor. What really caught my eye, however,

was this young man's reverence and humility as he lay there weeping and moving his lips to the worship songs. I was struck by his willingness to get on his face before God. And then as I preached, I could tell he was soaking up every word as he listened attentively and took notes.

When I finished speaking, I made a beeline to meet this young man who was obviously on fire for Jesus. I found out that his name is Justin Wren, and we spent a lot of time together that week. We connected so well, in fact, that I invited Justin to come and spend some time with me and my family, which he was glad to do.

After picking Justin up at the Charlotte airport and taking him to my house, I went to get us all something to eat. When I came back home I didn't see Justin, so I asked my wife where he was. Amy whispered to me to keep my voice down and to go look at the couch. There I saw this bear of a human being sprawled out asleep, with all three of my boys sleeping on his huge chest!

I have never met a young man who has such love for Jesus and other people. What really blows me away, though, are all the walls Justin has had to overcome in his life.

JUSTIN'S WALLS

His story begins in his home state of Texas, where the men are men and the steers are nervous. But this part of the country that is known for growing big, strong, and fearless men posed a problem early in Justin's life: He was constantly bullied for being overweight. After years of suffering abuse, Justin decided to check out the sport of wrestling and quickly discovered a great talent. Wrestling not only gave Justin a lot of confidence, it also brought him two state championships and one national title, followed by an invitation to live and train at the Olympic Training Center in Colorado Springs right out of high school.

Eventually Justin fell in love with mixed martial arts (MMA), the rapidly growing sport in which two men enter a caged ring and fight it out until one of them gives up or gets knocked out. MMA encompasses many different forms of fighting, such as Brazilian jujitsu, karate, boxing, Muay Thai, and wrestling. Athletes with a wrestling background tend to have an advantage, since nothing spells success like getting your opponent on the mat and doing damage. Because Justin was a big, strong, confident wrestler, it was no surprise that he was soon being looked at by the biggest company in the business, the Ultimate Fighting Championship (UFC).

Justin experienced a lot of success first in wrestling and then in the UFC, but that success came at the price of many painful injuries. Justin found himself addicted to alcohol, painkillers, marijuana, and other drugs as he tried to soothe his constant aches and pains. This young man who earlier had to break down a wall of depression and isolation as a result of being bullied was now fighting for his life as he ran up against a wall of addiction.

Eventually Justin's addictions led to something he wasn't accustomed to—losing in the ring. Justin continued to struggle both in and out of competition until a longtime friend shared the gospel with him and he gave his life to the Lord.

Not long after this was when I met Justin at the camp in Colorado. You could tell just by looking at his face that what he had was real. Justin would be tested, however, by the same MMA community that used to give him love. They heard reports that he had left MMA to become an evangelist and preach the gospel around the world. People are always scared of what they don't understand, so instead of supporting him they attacked him ruthlessly. He was blasted on MMA Web sites, on talk radio shows, at fight gyms where up and coming studs train to be the next great one, and even by some friends who didn't understand how he could give it all away.

Once again, Justin had another wall to knock down. After fighting for self-worth and overcoming addiction, now he was being persecuted for his faith.

JUSTIN'S CALLING

Justin kept moving forward and growing as a believer until he received what he considers his life calling from the Lord when he visited and saw the plight of the Mbuti Pygmies in the Democratic Republic of Congo. These seminomadic people not only have never heard of Jesus' love but are brutalized by other tribes. The Mbuti are forced into slavery to work the mines, and sometimes they are even victims of cannibalism because their oppressors believe they receive special spiritual powers from eating these small people. Justin saw the Mbuti Pygmies as the ultimate bullying victims, and the self-conscious thirteen-year-old boy inside of him could relate to them.

I can't even begin to imagine the horrors these poor people live with. But Justin couldn't imagine not going there to make a difference. So he returned to Africa and hiked deep into the Congo jungle, where the canopy is so thick you can't even see the sun, in order to share Jesus with this lost and needy tribe.

When Justin came back to the United States, he called to tell me one God story after another about how many of the Mbuti overcame the wall of sin and received Christ and how he was able to encourage the people to believe that their wall of slavery and persecution can fall as well. When they found out that the 6'4" Justin was a fighter, the Pygmies—most of whom are no taller than 4'9"—took blood from a fresh kill and poured it all over him, making him their head warrior! (Now that fits in well with the last chapter—Justin definitely got blood on him!) And the Pygmies gave Justin a new name: Instead of being called Justin Wren, he would now be called *Efeosa*, which means "The man who loves us."

Justin went on to tell me how he was adopted by the Pygmies and how he would be going back to live in a grass hut among them after raising fifty thousand dollars so that he can buy them out of slavery. Justin has overcome bullying, which can be so painful that it drives many teenagers in America to commit suicide. He has overcome drug and alcohol addiction, which I know from first-hand experience is no small feat. He has overcome professional failure and personal persecution, taking the freedom he received through Christ to the Congo in order to see freedom come to a tribe of Pygmies who call themselves "The Forgotten People." (If you want to learn more about Justin or support his advocacy efforts, visit his Web site: www.JustinTheVikingWren.com.)

Oh what God stories Justin will have to tell when he returns, and oh what a great mark he is making on the world. Though the mixed martial arts crowd may forget Justin "The Viking" Wren, a tribe in the Congo jungle will never forget Justin a.k.a. "Efeosa," the giant of a man who loves them and came to see their wall of physical and spiritual slavery fall down.

IT'S UP TO YOU

So what about you? Will you let any walls stand between you and the kind of relationship God yearns for you to have with Him? Will you let any walls stand between you and a life that makes a difference in the world and contributes to God's kingdom?

The choice is yours. I pray that you and I will choose to see our walls fall down so that we can experience true freedom in Christ and help others to do the same.

Let's get it on!